End Times Evangelism

The Bible Explains the News

Scott Huckaby

ISBN: 1508674892
ISBN-13: 978-1508674894

For information regarding author interviews,
please contact Scott Huckaby via his blog:
newswisdom.blogspot.com

ABOUT THE COVER

"For as the lightning comes from the east and flashes to the west, so also will the coming of the Son of Man be."
(Matthew 24:27)

Jesus Christ first came to earth as the Lamb of God to show us God's love and establish His Spiritual Kingdom. He is returning as the Lion of Judah to conclude God's wrath of the Tribulation and establish His Millennial Kingdom. The Lord's return to earth from heaven will be sudden and visible to all as lightning flashes in the sky. Church Age followers of Jesus will accompany Him when he returns. We have a great opportunity and duty to help others know the good news about Jesus as our Savior before it is too late.

Photograph of monsoon storm over Alpine, Texas
by Teresa Huckaby, www.windriverfoto.com

DEDICATED TO:

My rocket-scientist father-in-law Jim Miller who planted seeds by sharing his love of Bible prophecy with me; and to the beautiful love of my life, best friend, editor and wife Teresa Huckaby who watered the seeds of Bible prophecy with our many conversations about current events.

"I planted, Apollos watered, but God gave the increase"
(1 Corinthians 3:6)

CONTENTS

INTRODUCTION

Scott Huckaby's Testimony

God used His prophetic Word to open my heart to Him. This convinced me that others can similarly come to know Jesus Christ as their Savior and Lord. I have found through my own friendship evangelism that discussing God's prophetic Word does resonate as being powerful in people. My strong conviction about the power of Bible prophesy is what led me to develop this book; to serve as a resource for fellow news junkies to help others relate what is going on in the world to what God told us will soon happen in His Word. This is particularly important in the stage of history that we find ourselves.

Before I personally got to know Jesus, I was raised in the church and spent a big part of my life appearing to be and even considering myself to be a Christian. But I was really only a cultural Christian who never gave a lot of thought to what happens after a person dies. My reasoning was that if this material world is all we can be sure about then spending time on spiritual matters is a waste of time.

Soon after I was married, my father-in-law gave me a book he had read called, "The End of the Days" by Arthur E. Bloomfield. It was a book on Bible prophecy which I considered to be a crack-pot concept but it intrigued me because I was drawn to the post-apocalyptic Sci-Fi genre.

The "End of the Days" was essentially a commentary on the biblical writings of the Prophet Daniel. I was impressed with the straight-forward systematic approach the book took to interpreting Scripture; basically it took Scripture literally while recognizing obvi-

1

ous symbolic language that is common to any good literature.

I read this commentary on Daniel about the time the Berlin wall came down at the end of 1989. The demise of the Soviet Union perplexed me because I had grown up in a world where the superpower standoff between the U.S. and Soviet Union was the natural order of things. Indeed, I had spent nine years of my life training for war with the Soviet Union as a U.S. Army officer. The claims that it was time to cash in our peace dividends didn't make sense because all those nukes still existed and at least half of them were in the hands of people who had to be reeling from their loss of power.

The book of Daniel has prophecies of the nations that would rule the world from Israel's perspective beginning with the Babylonian Empire until the Messiah returns. These prophecies are in such detail that I became convinced the Bible had to be from God because only He can *"declare the end from the beginning"* (Isaiah 46:10).

What happened to the Soviet Union could be explained by Bible prophecy; the superpower stand-off had to be resolved to make way for the world-wide government that will be in place when the Messiah returns.

As I discussed these things with my wife Teresa one evening it occurred to me, if the Bible could help me understand the reason current events happened the way they did, it had to also be right about the need to have Jesus in my life. It was like a light going on in my head; if I didn't start following Jesus at that moment, I knew I was going to spend eternity separated from Him in hell. It was a classic "no brainer"; I immediately committed to studying the Bible to learn more about Jesus so that I could follow Him.

Since I have had Jesus in my life, He has helped me change my worldview from a materialistic perspective to His eternal perspective; and this has helped me deal with various difficulties in life as well as all the craziness that is so pervasive in the world today.

The biggest struggle I've had with my faith resulted in my greatest growth spurt. The conventional wisdom of evolutionary science bothered me because it conflicted with the literal biblical account of creation. Then I discovered the great blessing of creation science. There really is an abundance of physical evidence that reinforces a literal interpretation of Genesis. Through this, I learned that God so desired a personal relationship with me that I could trust the plain sense meaning of His Word. This energized my personal Bible study knowing I was not dependant on some scholarly intermediary to tell me what God really said.

There are a lot of similarities between the event God used to wake me up to Him and what is going on now. Today, we have the global problems of the economy, terrorism and climate change. These issues are too big for any one nation to fix; it requires the co-operation of the whole world. As the U.S./Soviet superpower stand off had to be resolved, so too does the last remaining superpower have to yield its sovereignty to the world community of nations. It is painful to consider this but it is hard to see how the U.S. can come out of the current political, economic and societal problems with the superpower clout we once had.

The prophecies of the Bible reveal we are on the cusp of some dramatic changes. The greatest sign we are living in the time prior to the Messiah coming is seen in the prophecies about Israel coming back together as a nation after close to 1900 years of being dispersed among the nations of the world. Bible prophecy proves that Scripture is God's revelation of Himself to mankind. Only God can tell us with 100% accuracy what will happen in the future because He is outside the confines of time. Time is simply a fourth dimension of our world that God created along with the physical characteristics of the universe.

As an electrical engineer with a love for math and science, I have always been analytical in my faith. To me, faith in Jesus Christ is logical. God gave us the ability to reason and He wants us to use our cognitive abilities to know Him. As He said in Isaiah 1:18, *"Come now, and let us reason together."*

Indeed, a logical approach to things is what led the French mathematician Blaise Pascal to Christ. Pascal was the father of statistical science which he applied to the truth about God. "Pascal's Wager" is quite profound; it essentially asks us to weigh the upside against the downside of believing the Bible assuming it really does turn out to be from God. Betting against the Bible being true has the severest of consequences while wagering that the Bible is true leads to eternal blessings. It is simply illogical not to *"taste and see that the Lord is good"* as Psalm 34:8 invites us to do.

The Bible is the most important resource we have in this world; life would be just plain scary without it.

1 USING THIS BOOK

This book is a resource to help Christians relate current events to the Bible using God's prophetic Word as a powerful evangelistic tool. Lives are changed when people recognize the supernatural nature of the Bible revealed through fulfilled prophecies. Also, as we see the stage being set for future prophecies to be fulfilled, it gives us a sense of urgency to grow closer to Jesus Christ and share the good news about Him. Indeed, God revealed the future to us for just that purpose: *"the testimony of Jesus is the spirit of prophecy"* (Revelation 19:10). The Church generally does not use God's prophetic Word for evangelism. This book will help Christians take advantage of such missed opportunities.

Readers of this book should gain confidence in using God's prophetic Word to help others better understand God's plan. Chapters 2 and 3 of this book address fundamentals of prophecy to help the reader be better equipped to say why they believe what they believe in the spirit of 1 Peter 3:15: *"always be ready to give a defense to everyone who asks you a reason for the hope that is in you, with meekness and fear."*

Chapter 4 to the end of the book includes some more category-specific background but is primarily a collection of brief commentaries with a relevant Scripture passage on topics likely to come up when discussing current events. These topical commentaries are in a logical order of progression to help readers develop their prophetic biblical worldview. These chapters may also be used as reference to better recognize the prophetic significance of a particular development in the news.

1.1 Conversational Evangelism

Most people we encounter don't know Jesus Christ as their Savior, much less their Lord, *"because narrow is the gate and difficult is the way which leads to life, and there are few who find it"* (Matthew 7:14). This makes the world a dark place and means we are in a target rich environment for people who need to know the Lord. However, it is discouraging to present the good news of Christ to people before they have been prepared by the Holy Spirit; *"do not give what is holy to the dogs; nor cast your pearls before swine, lest they trample them under their feet, and turn and tear you in pieces"* (Matthew 7:6).

A much better approach to evangelism is to apply what Jesus said we should be doing: *"Let your light so shine before men, that they may see your good works and glorify your Father in heaven"* (Matthew 5:16). We let our light shine in this dark world when we let those around us know we are followers of Jesus Christ. A good way to do that is to salt our speech during the course of normal conversation with "faith flags" which are favorable references to Jesus, the Bible, Church, prayer, or other things that reveal our biblical worldview. Then we should just live our lives applying the principles God has given us in His Word.

As our associates recognize us as Christians, they'll be watching to see if there is anything different about us. Hopefully, they'll observe spiritual fruit in our lives per Galatians 5:22-23. For example, they may see that we have a *"peace of God, which surpasses all understanding"* in the midst of circumstances which are hardly peaceful (Philippians 4:7). God can use that to attract people to Him. As unbelievers observe us, they may notice we have something in our lives they wish they had. And if they associate what we have as being due to our relationship to Jesus, they become more open to Him.

God created us to need Him in our lives (John 17:3). People know deep down in their heart of hearts there is something wrong if they do not have an active relationship with Jesus. Often we try to fill that relationship void with things of this world but nothing satisfies like Jesus. The Holy Spirit convicts people that what we really need in our lives is a relationship with Jesus (John 16:8-9). The Holy Spirit does all the heavy lifting in bringing people to Christ, all we have to do is be available to answer the questions of those seeking to know Him. And they will ask us questions if they know we are Christians when they respond to the Holy Spirit. We know people are truly ready to hear the good news about Jesus by the questions they ask.

A great "faith flag" to plant while discussing current events is what the Bible says about the news. This is very relevant because people are increasingly concerned about trends in the world. It is not hard to see that we are rapidly headed toward a culmination of history. The more people come to see how the Bible helps us make sense of these perplexing events, the more they become open to Christ. This book will help Christians lead conversations about current events from a biblical perspective with those who express interest by their questions.

God commands His followers in the Great Commission to be His representative on earth to help others know Him (Matthew 28:19-20). As we see the Day Jesus will return drawing near, it should give us a sense of urgency to do what we can to be a part of what God is doing in the hearts of others. As Jesus said, *"I must work the works of Him who sent Me while it is day; the night is coming when no one can work"* (John 9:4). Our freedom to tell people about Jesus will some day be taken away; we should take advantage of this blessing while it is available to us.

1.2 Relating Any News to the Bible

Users of this book should find themselves getting better at figuring out what is really going on in a news story in order to relate it to Bible prophecy. Current events often represent some trend that is disturbing if you consider where it is taking us. Also, there is usually an agenda behind what is being reported on that can be discerned with just a little practice looking critically at the news. But End Time Evangelists should not think they are limited to the topics addressed in this book. Any news story may be used to point people to Scripture even if they don't appear to be related to some aspect of Bible prophecy. The following are some general categories about news stories; every news report is guaranteed to apply to at least one of these topics.

1.3 A Great Achievement

Every good gift and every perfect gift is from above,
and comes down from the Father of lights (James 1:17)

Sometimes there is good news reported and when it is, this is cause for rejoicing. We should praise God when we hear a good report because it is from Him that all blessings flow. Often these stories give the glory to the people involved and we should praise those who demonstrated godly characteristics to make great achievements. But we should not lose sight of who is behind all greatness. It is God who gives us our abilities, inspiration, and opportunities. *"Having then gifts differing according to the grace that is given to us, let us use them"* (Romans 12:6).

1.4 Human Interest Stories

Whatever things are true, whatever things are noble, whatever things are just, whatever things are pure, whatever things are lovely, whatever things are of good report, if there is any virtue and if there is anything praiseworthy-- meditate on these things (Philippians 4:8)

News agencies must feel guilty having to report so much bad news all the time so they often include what is referred to as a human interest story. These stories are easy for people to identify with because they relate experiences that are common to the human condition. But what makes these stories heartwarming? They generally point us to values that God has wired every person to appreciate. We are made in the image of God to see the merits of the same things He does (Genesis 1:27). So the next time we're blessed by a news story, we should praise our Creator who gave us His values.

1.5 Bad News

Evil men and impostors will grow worse and worse, deceiving and being deceived (2 Timothy 3:13)

People lament that the only news that gets reported is bad news. Certainly there is more bad news than good and this is a trend that will continue until the Lord returns. Society will degenerate even more as we get closer to the return of Christ. God is removing His restraint of evil as a birth pang of the coming Kingdom of Christ on earth. There will be no restraint of evil during the seven years preceding the return of Jesus when mankind will have free reign to pursue a utopian vision of life apart from the God of the Bible. The ultimate evil man called the Antichrist will lead the world in this futile quest that will end at Armageddon and the return of Jesus.

1.6 Tragic News

We know that all things work together for good to those who love God,
to those who are the called according to His purpose (Romans 8:28)

Most bad news does not impact us personally, but when something does, it rises to the level of a tragedy. Sometimes we know why bad things are happening to us and we can learn a lesson from them to avoid such problems in the future. But often there is no good reason why the righteous suffer. We often question our omnipotent God why He would allow this tragedy in our lives. Since God is in control, it is right to question what purpose He has for our circumstances. He has promised to give us His wisdom if we ask for it in James 1:5. God always does bring something beneficial from even the bad things that happen to us. We may not realize it while in our mortal bodies but can be assured that we'll recognize it when we're resurrected. The value in personal tragedy may be to help us pause from our busy lives to draw closer to God; or to help us see the need to depend on Him and His limitless resources rather than our own meager abilities. He may be putting us through our difficulties just to prepare us to help someone else in a similar situation which He can use to attract them to Him.

1.7 Disaster News

God will wipe away every tear from their eyes; there shall be no more death,
nor sorrow, nor crying. There shall be no more pain, for the former things
have passed away (Revelation 21:4)

When we hear news of disaster or some incident demonstrating the depravity of mankind, it should bring to mind how desperately this world needs the return of the Lord. We can encourage others by telling them how we are looking forward to the return of the Messiah who will bring justice to this world so that there will only be good news. This attracts people to the Savior because everyone grows weary of bad news whether they admit it or not.

1.8 God's Judgment in Disaster

Do you suppose that these Galileans were worse sinners than all other
Galileans, because they suffered such things? I tell you, no; but unless
you repent you will all likewise perish. (Luke 13:2-3)

Disasters can occur as a consequence for a nation offending God by bringing harm to Israel (Genesis 12:3). But in general, disasters do not occur due to the sinfulness of a nation because all nations are sinful. We live in a fallen world where disasters happen indiscriminately; *"He makes His sun rise on the evil and on the good, and sends rain on the just and on the unjust"* (Matthew 5:45). So from a spiritual standpoint, all disasters do is to shake up the spiritually discerning to get closer to God and that is something we all need from time to time.

1.9 Dealing with Bad News

Yet to all who received him, to those who believed in his name,
he gave the right to become children of God (John 1:12, NIV)

Christians shouldn't be distressed by bad news reports. If you have allowed Jesus Christ to be the Lord of your life, you are part of God's family. As part of God's family, we will be spending eternity with Him and what happens in this life will be insignificant in light of eternity. Bad news reminds us how messed up this world is and how badly it needs Jesus Christ to return. It also helps to remember that we are but sojourners in this world, *"our citizenship is in heaven"* (Philippians 3:20).

1.10 Fearful News

God has not given us a spirit of fear, but of power
and of love and of a sound mind (2 Timothy 1:7)

The trends of this world are often apparent in news reports for those who honestly consider their implications. Most people don't give much thought to current events because it only makes their fears grow. Knowing Jesus as Lord is the best way to cope because He helps us face our fears with a sound, rational mind and is a by-product of having a personal relationship with Him.

1.11 Desiring the Return of Christ

He will have no fear of bad news; his heart is steadfast,
trusting in the LORD (Psalm 112:7, NIV)

The follower of Christ need not fear news reports, no matter how bad they are. We know that the Lord is in control and that He loves His children. All bad news reports really do is remind us how sorely this world needs Jesus to return. And as we see the trends developing, we get a sense for how close we are to our *"blessed hope"* (Titus 2:13). God will use our courage in the face of bad news reports to attract others to Him.

2 END TIMES CONTROVERSY

This chapter discusses why there is so much confusion from various interpretations of Scripture and advocates taking the text as literally as possible to avoid such problems. The reasons the Church generally avoids Bible prophecy are addressed and a case is made for why this should change. A discussion of heaven is included because common misconceptions about it contribute to people neglecting Bible prophecy.

2.1 Biblical Authority

Bible skeptics often cite the fact that Scripture is subject to interpretation as reason to dismiss it as the Word of God. Indeed, that is why we have so many different Christian denominations. The fact that Christians generally agree on the fundamentals such as who Jesus is and why He came does not carry any weight with those who seek to discredit the authority of Scripture.

The Bible skeptics do however have something of a point; if Scripture is subject to divergent interpretations then its value as the authority of God has to be suspect. There is a big difference between viewing the Bible as God's inspired message to mankind versus the story of man's search for God. If the Bible is merely the story of man's search for God then it is bound to have myths and unreliable information about God because man is flawed. But if our Creator God is truly Almighty and loves us enough to reveal Himself to us in the person of Jesus Christ, then He surely provided a means by which we can know Him. He has, by sending us the Holy Spirit who helps us to understand the Holy Scriptures (2 Corinthians 2:9-14).

God explained how His Word was given to us when He inspired the Apostle Peter to write that, *"no prophecy of Scripture is of any private interpretation, for prophecy never came by the will of man, but holy men of God spoke as they were moved by the Holy Spirit"* (2 Peter 1:20-21). In the several verses preceding this passage, Peter recalled his experience of seeing the glorified Jesus on the Mount of Transfiguration. Essentially, Peter said that Scripture was more reliable than his own personal experiences. He recognized that our experiences can be deceptive. Peter could have had some kind of hallucinogenic plant in his lunch salad without realizing it and imagined his whole experience on the Mount of Transfiguration. On the other hand, God is Almighty and will not allow false words to represent Him in something as important as the Holy Bible.

2.2 Doctrines of Demons

God gave us His Word so that His followers may authenticate what is truly from Him and what is a deception that lures people away from Him. As the Church Age comes to a close, there has been an increasing influence of demonic doctrines that just don't square with Scripture (see 1 Timothy 4:1). Some popular doctrines that demons have no-doubt inspired which God's people need to be well grounded in Scripture to recognize are as follows:

- Many have been deceived to believe that all religions really worship the same God. For example, anyone doing more than a superficial comparison will find that the Islamic moon god Allah is not the God of the Bible.
- There is a misguided belief there are many paths to heaven; following Jesus is just one of them. Believing this turns Jesus into a liar. In John 14:6 Jesus said, *"I am the way, the truth, and the life. No one comes to the Father except through Me."*
- Demons have inspired wrong ideas about Jesus that either deny His deity or humanity. The Bible clearly reveals both His deity and humanity.
- Many have embraced the lies that deny certain fundamental facts about Jesus like His virgin birth, sinless life and physical resurrection; they just don't believe the testimony of Scripture.

- All human developed religions believe the false doctrine that salvation may be earned by one's good works; Ephesians 2:8-9 could not be clearer in telling us this can not be the case.
- Many have bought into the erroneous idea that a person can lose their salvation; this is really salvation by works since if you can do anything to lose your salvation, then salvation has to be dependent on one's works.

If people believe God's Word, there is no way they can accept any of these false doctrines.

2.3 Disputable Matters

There is another category of disagreement among Bible-believing Christians which was called *"disputes over doubtful things"* in Romans 14:1. Disputable matters are convictions that have nothing to do with a person's salvation. Examples are infant baptism, use of instruments in praise music, dancing, drinking, gambling, smoking, etcetera. The Apostle Paul recognized that differences in spiritual growth can result in people having different convictions about issues not explicitly addressed in Scripture. In Romans 14, Paul encourages the more spiritual believer to yield to the convictions of the less mature Christian. It is interesting that most people will assume it is always the other person who is the least spiritually mature and thus should be the one to accommodate the other's convictions. This recognizes our human nature and helps us do the right thing in the knowledge that only God can correctly judge a person's spiritual growth.

As the Church Age has progressed, disputable matters have been made more pronounced by divergent views of Scripture. The believer who thinks the Bible is the story of man's search for God will tend to have different interpretations from those who think of Scripture as God's inspired Word. The believer who takes a more literal view of Scripture will have a different view from those who believe certain categories of Scripture only have value representing spiritual truths. The danger with liberal interpretations of Scripture is that this makes it all too easy to compromise with the world. And there is a lot of compromise with the world going on in the Church today; *"the time will come when they will not endure sound doctrine, but according to their own desires, because they have itching ears, they will heap up for themselves teachers; and they will turn their ears away from the truth, and be turned aside to fables"* (1 Timothy 4:3-4).

13

The damage that liberal interpretations of Scripture do to God's Word is to bolster the false idea that the Bible is unreliable as our premier source of authority. So the best policy for the believer is to recognize the authority of Scripture as being God's Word to us and take it literally unless it is obviously symbolic (2 Timothy 3:16-17). As prophecy teacher David Reagan likes to say, "When the plain sense makes sense, seek no other sense or you'll end up with nonsense."

2.4 Reducing Disputability

The more Christians agree on a less liberal and more conservative, literal view of Scripture, the fewer disputable matters we would have in the Church. This would go a long way toward demonstrating unity in the Body of Christ giving less ammunition to those seeking to discredit God's Word.

The question of literal interpretation has direct relevance to the important disputable matter of the end times. There are divergent views in eschatology, the study of the end times. Most professing Christians have an amillennial view that there will be no literal 1,000-year reign of Christ on earth. They believe all end times events happen in conjunction with Jesus returning to immediately usher in the Eternal State. While this view is attractive because of its perceived simplicity, it forces us to have to see the prophetic Word as speaking only of spiritual matters without having a literal meaning. The problem with that is the prophecies of Jesus coming the first time were literally fulfilled, so why shouldn't we view those of His return the same way?

All biblical scholars who take the most literal view of Scripture have a futurist, premillennial view of eschatology believing Jesus will literally fulfill His promise of a 1,000-year physical kingdom on earth before the Eternal State begins. Thus, the premillennial view is the more correct because the more literal view of Scripture is actually the simpler interpretation. While the amillennial view appears to be simple, it presents significant interpretation problems in forcing adherents to come up with a spiritual or allegorical meaning for all the rich details given in most Bible prophecies. It is much simpler to take the text literally believing it means what it says.

Most Christians seem to avoid studying the book of Revelation beyond Chapter 3 saying it is just too hard to understand. It certainly is hard to understand if you have to spiritualize everything that it says. The problem amillennialists have with the book of Revelation is not that it is too hard to understand, it is too hard for them to believe. There is way too much rich detail in the book of Revelation than should be there if the only message we are to take from it is the spiritual concept that there is a struggle between good and evil with Christ winning in the end.

It is interesting to note that most people who believe we should only make spiritual interpretations of Bible prophecy also have the same view of Genesis. Theistic evolution is the idea that God used an evolutionary process to bring about the creation. While this idea is within the pale of orthodoxy, it is also a gross compromise with the world by Christians who don't want to be branded as being unscientific. To believe that God used an evolutionary process to create mankind requires a non-literal interpretation of Scripture. The Bible says there was no death before the original sin but evolution requires survival of the fittest which involves many cycles of death. God goes out of His way describing the six days of creation as being 24-hour days as we know them making reference to morning and evening on each day; day-ages have no morning and evening.

There is a lot more that can be said of the problems with amillennialism and theistic evolution but that is beyond the scope of this book. However, there will be some who ask:

2.5 Why does it Matter?

Why do differences in our understanding of beginning things and ending things matter so long as we can agree on the fundamentals? When Scripture does not mean what is says in Genesis and Revelation, it sows a seed of doubt on everything in between. *"If they do not hear Moses and the prophets, neither will they be persuaded though one rise from the dead"* (Luke 16:29). Well One did return from the dead and most people do not believe His testimony. God doesn't want us to have to wonder if John 3:16 may be taken literally or only has some subtle spiritualized meaning. Thank God John 3:16 means what it says.

Always having to "interpret" some spiritualized meaning for Scripture makes followers of Christ dependant on specially anointed scholars to tell us what God is really saying in His Word. Why bother to study God's Word for yourself if you need some specially trained expert to interpret God's Word for us? It dilutes the plan of God for

Christ's followers to have personal relationships with Him if we must have intermediaries to tell us what God is saying to us. Such a belief creates unhealthy dependencies that cult leaders exploit. Instead, we should embrace the priesthood of the believer taught in 1 Peter 2:5-9 recognizing, *"there is one God and one Mediator between God and men, the Man Christ Jesus"* (1 Timothy 2:5).

If Satan and his minions were to devise a strategy to dumb-down Christians, can you think of any better way to do it than convince us that God's Word does not really mean what it says? Indeed, Satan did just that when he tempted Eve in the Garden of Eden (Genesis 3:1-5).

There is a warning in Scripture about neglecting the full meaning of God's prophetic Word: *"If anyone adds to these things, God will add to him the plagues that are written in this book; and if anyone takes away from the words of the book of this prophecy, God shall take away his part from the Book of Life, from the holy city, and from the things which are written in this book"* (Revelation 22:18-19). Isn't denying the plain sense meaning of certain portions of the book of Revelation taking away from what is written in it?

There will be loss of reward for those who take a lazy view of Scripture and depend on others to give them a spiritual interpretation while ignoring the literal meaning. Thus it would behoove us all to, *"be diligent to present yourself approved to God, a worker who does not need to be ashamed, rightly dividing the word of truth"* (2 Timothy 2:15).

2.6 Avoiding Bible Prophecy

Many people believe the Bible to be God's Word, but they can't give unbelievers a very convincing reason for why they believe that. Telling an unbeliever that the Bible is just something Christians must take on faith is weak. Our faith that the Bible is God's Word is not blind faith. God gave us an ability to reason and He wants us to use that capacity to know the truth (Isaiah 1:18). A working understanding of Bible prophecy will help people see a good *"reason for the hope"* that is within us (1 Peter 3:15).

Among the many reasons we know the Bible is from God is that it foretells future events with 100% accuracy. Only God can do this because only He is beyond the confines of time (Isaiah 46:9-10). It is surely one of the strategies of the devil that most professing Christians ignore the prophetic aspects of God's Word. This is a tragedy because it causes people to miss out on an important way to know our Lord.

Another reason we should study Bible prophecy is given in 2 Timothy 3:16 which says that all Scripture is inspired by God. This means we should use all of Scripture. Anything less is like a V-8 engine missing a couple spark plugs (it puts out a lot of noise but has no power if it runs at all). There are more prophetic verses in the Bible than those addressing the important doctrines of salvation, faith, blood atonement for sin, and many others. Over 28% of the verses in the Old Testament and 21% of the New Testament present prophetic material.

Bible prophecy reveals who Christ is: *"the testimony of Jesus is the spirit of prophecy"* (Revelation 19:10). Studying Bible Prophecy is a critical part of learning about Jesus. There are over 300 prophecies in the Old Testament concerning the first coming of Christ which were all fulfilled by Him. As scientist Peter Stoner determined, if only 7 of the prophecies of Christ's first advent had happened accidentally, this is a probability of one chance in a hundred-quadrillion, about the number of silver dollars it would take to cover Texas knee deep.

There are over 500 prophecies of Christ's second coming in the Old Testament. And 1 out of every 25 verses in the New Testament pertains to His return. More of Scripture is dedicated to Christ's Second Advent because He is coming in wrath this time and God wants His people to be ready.

2.7 Dispensationalism
Jesus Christ is the same yesterday, today, and forever (Hebrews 13:8)
Scholars who take the Bible literally expect Jesus to physically rule on earth for 1,000 years (Revelation 20:4). This time period is referred to as the dispensation of the Millennial Kingdom. A dispensation is a period of time where God deals with mankind in a different way from other periods of time.

Amillennialists love to malign dispensationalists as not being biblical because of Hebrews 13:8. But you don't have to be a specially trained theologian to recognize that God has indeed dealt with mankind differently in history. Compare the Dispensation of the Law in Old Testament times with the Dispensation of Grace during the Church Age. Jesus distinguished the two dispensations when He initiated a New Covenant with the Church (Luke 22:20). Those in Old

Testament times who would spend eternity with their Creator did their best to observe God's Law having to admit that they were powerless to meet God's standard of perfection (Matthew 5:48). So Old Testament believers had to trust in the unmerited favor of God having faith in His provision of the Messiah who would deliver them.

In this Age of Grace, we are saved the same way Old Testament believers were, by grace through faith (Ephesians 2:8-9). But we also have a much better understanding of how God made it possible for our sins to be forgiven in Jesus sacrificing His life for us on the cross (Romans 5:8). While salvation is the same now as during the Dispensation of the Law, God worked through Israel to reveal Himself to mankind and faith was demonstrated by doing one's best to observe the Law. In the current Dispensation of Grace, God is working through the Church as His representative on earth and faith is demonstrated by following our Savior Jesus Christ.

2.8 Commanded to Watch

Another good reason to study Bible prophecy is that we are commanded to watch for Christ's coming: *"watch therefore, and pray always that you may be counted worthy to escape all these things that will come to pass, and to stand before the Son of Man"* (Luke 21:36). One can not watch for Jesus without knowing His prophetic Word. It is necessary to know what to look for to recognize the prophetic implication of current events. As we see developments indicating the return of the Lord is near, we get excited about it and this infectiously attracts people to Jesus.

It is important to note that watching for the Lord is not the same as waiting for Him. Consider a case where a sailor came home from a long voyage and noted with disappointment that his wife was not among those watching for their husbands on the pier. When he went to his house, his wife met him at the door saying she had been waiting for him. The sailor replied that he would much rather she had been watching for him instead. Waiting is passive; watching is active. Waiting can be done while doing something else making it a low-priority activity. Watching requires one's full attention with interest in all aspects of Who we're watching for and shows love with action.

There is danger in not watching for the Lord. Jesus said, *"if you will not watch, I will come upon you as a thief"* (Revelation 3:3). Jesus doesn't want us to be surprised by His coming which will rob us of blessings He has in mind for us. He does not want us to be caught unaware and not ready for His return. If we do not love the Lord enough to watch for Him, we have to question our salvation. Those who are not anxiously looking for the return of Jesus are no better than unbelievers who scoff at the idea Jesus will return (1 Thessalonians 5:2-3).

Being watchful is acknowledging that all things will not continue as they have from the beginning (2 Peter 3:4). It includes believing Jesus when He said, *"the end will come"* (Matthew 24:14); and applying that understanding to our lives so that we prepare for eternity. If a person thinks they have their whole lifetime to get on-board with what God is calling them to do, it is easy to put it off until it never happens. But if the Rapture is imminent as Scripture teaches, then there is an urgency to at least get started on what God has called us to do.

We should also be engaged in watching for Jesus because it is a great blessing to us in the here and now as well as in eternity. Revelation 22:7 says, *"Blessed is he who keeps the words of the prophecy of this book"* (see also Revelation 1:2). Seeing the evil trends in this world is pretty depressing. But knowing that Christ and His followers win in the end helps us to deal with whatever this world throws at us. Such an eternal perspective is a blessing that enables us to have joy despite our circumstances.

Embracing the doctrine of the imminent Rapture is an essential part of watching for Christ. Knowing that we could find ourselves in the presence of our Lord before our next breath gives us additional incentive to, *"live soberly, righteously, and godly in the present age, looking for the blessed hope and glorious appearing of our great God and Savior Jesus Christ"* (Titus 2:12-13). If we really think the Rapture could happen at any time, we should not want to be in the midst of doing something we'd be ashamed of before our Lord. Looking for our *"blessed hope"* means we should live holy lives being ready for the Rapture at any time. So being watchful is a powerful catalyst for sanctification (1 John 3:2-3).

Watching for Jesus means we are anticipating His judgment. *"It is appointed unto men once to die, but after this the judgment"* (Hebrews 9:27). Being watchful means knowing we're accountable to our Lord for how we live our lives. Preparing for meeting our Lord means that we should adopt an eternal perspective which helps us make wise decisions in the here and now. It is wise to prepare for what comes after this life and the sooner we start doing that, the more blessings we'll enjoy in eternity.

There will be rewards for being watchful, *"there is laid up for me the crown of righteousness, which the Lord, the righteous Judge, will give to me on that Day, and not to me only but also to all who have loved His appearing"* (2 Timothy 4:8). Jesus said that rewards in heaven are something we should seek in Matthew 6:20. He also told us in His parable of the talents that the nature of our rewards will be greater authority in His Kingdom (Matthew 25:14-30). God will be doing amazing things in eternity and we should want to be as much a part of that as we can.

Being watchful involves doing what God has called us to do before it is too late. We should take full advantage of the opportunities we have to represent our Lord; the day is coming when we will no longer be able to warn the lost (John 9:4). God will save whom He will save but blesses us when we allow Him to use us. We should not want to miss out on any blessings God has planned for us.

We should watch for Jesus because He gave us the signs to watch for in His Olivet Discourse, Matthew 24 and Luke 21. Being aware of these signs enough to recognize them and share them with others honors Him. And we are blessed in the process because God uses such fellowship to bring us closer to Him. Knowing the correct order of end times events helps us to not fear what appears to be developing because He said, *"See that you are not troubled; for all these things must come to pass, but the end is not yet"* (Matthew 24:6). As followers of Christ in the Church Age, we will see the birth pangs of the Tribulation but will not have to go through the Tribulation ourselves. It is a great blessing knowing that the Rapture precedes the Tribulation.

God praises those who are watchful enough to use His Word for understanding the times in which we are living. For example, He recognized, *"the children of Issachar who had understanding of the times, to know what Israel ought to do"* (1 Chronicles 12:32). And Jesus rebuked those who could not discern the signs of the times; He said, *"Hypocrites! You know how to discern the face of the sky, but you cannot discern the signs of the times"* (Matthew 16:3). While Jesus said this in relation to His First Advent, it applies to His Second Advent as well.

We should live our lives watching for Jesus because we don't know exactly when He is coming. *"Watch therefore, for you know neither the day nor the hour in which the Son of Man is coming"* (Matthew 25:13). While we can know the general season for the Rapture of the Church (1 Thessalonians 5:4), we can not be sure exactly when it will happen. This is by design; Jesus wants us to live our lives being ready for His return as He illustrated in the parable of the Wise Virgins, Matthew 25:1-13.

2.9 Excuses for Neglecting Prophecy

With all these good reasons to study Bible prophecy, why do most professing Christians avoid it? One reason people often give is that it involves too much doom and gloom. The prophets of Old Testament times were persecuted for proclaiming disaster for Israel so today's preachers generally avoid such uncomfortable prophetic topics. While Christ came in love, kindness and mercy the first time, He will be returning in judgment and wrath with fire and brimstone and multitudes dying. But the good news is that the follower of Christ during the current Church Age need not worry about the terrible time of God's wrath. Jesus will conclude the Church Age prior to the Tribulation with the resurrection of all believers living and dead at the Rapture. The future should be frightening for the unsaved. Fear of going to hell is healthy because it should bring us to Christ for salvation (Proverbs 19:23). If a person believes they are saved by their works, they don't want the Lord to come on one of their bad days. However if you know you are saved by grace, there are no "bad days."

Bible prophecy has gotten a bad name because of cults and self-proclaimed prophets who have distorted the Word of God to serve their own purposes. Thus some churches avoid Bible prophecy out of fear of being thought of as a cult. This is a plot by Satan to deceive mankind. False prophets and even sincere Christians have been coerced by Satan and his minions into setting dates for Christ's return. These dates have always come and gone only to damage the credibility of Bible prophecy. Date setters ignore what Jesus said in Matthew 24:36: *"of that day and hour no one knows."*

Others say that since we can not know when Christ will return, why does it matter? While we can not know the exact day Christ will return, we can know the general time-frame. Jesus gave us signs to help us watch for Him and Hebrews 10:24-25 tells us we can see the Day approaching, *"And let us consider one another in order to stir up love and good works, not forsaking the assembling of ourselves together, as is the manner of some, but exhorting one another, and so much the more as you see the Day approaching."*

The fact that Bible prophecy is ignored today is in itself prophetic (2 Peter 3:3-6). We are living in the age of scoffers who have forgotten that God judged the world once before in the flood and He will do so again. Liberal Christians deny that the Lord will physically return or believe His return has to be in the far distant future. They reason that if God used evolution to bring about the creation then it took millions of years for Christ to come the first time and could take millions of years for Him to return.

Some avoid Bible prophecy because they think it is too controversial and its proponents are too dogmatic. This criticism is usually from those who think we should not be dogmatic about anything because doctrine is divisive. But Bible doctrine is intended to divide, see Hebrews 4:12. Jesus said He did not come to bring peace on the earth but to set His people against those who need Him (Matthew 10:34-36).

There certainly is doctrine we should be dogmatic about: our sin nature, the Deity of Christ, His death atoning for the sins of those who trust in Him, His resurrection, the need to be born again, and once saved - always saved just to name a few. Likewise, we should also be dogmatically opposed to false doctrines which lead people away from Christ. One false doctrine involving Bible prophecy is that the Church will have to go through the time of God's wrath with the rest of humanity. This wrong teaching causes people to look for the coming of the Antichrist rather than the Lord. It can lead to excessive separation from the world where modern conveniences are shunned or a survivalist mentality develops where "enduring to the end" means stocking up and arming up to save oneself.

Some people avoid studying Bible prophecy because they think it is too escapist, too other-worldly, or too pie in the sky. These people think we should only study what will help us now, in this world. As Christians, we are called to keep our minds on the spiritual ramifications of what we do in this world: *"If then you were raised with Christ, seek those things which are above, where Christ is, sitting at the right hand of God. Set your mind on things above, not on things on the earth"* (Colossians 3:1-2). Our response to what will soon happen has a great bearing on how we act in the "here and now".

2.10 Misconceptions of Heaven

How a person feels about the return of Jesus tells a lot about their spiritual condition. The biggest reason people don't get excited about the soon return of Jesus is that they don't have a relationship with Him. But that doesn't mean they shouldn't consider His return. Indeed, the more a person comes to realize we truly are getting close to the return of Jesus, the more they will come under conviction to let Jesus into their life.

The next biggest reason people don't get excited about the soon return of Jesus is because they are harboring some misconceptions about heaven. The conventional wisdom about heaven is that it is an ethereal spirit world with no relation to our current physical existence. That couldn't be further from the truth. People have a triune body, soul, and spirit (1 Thessalonians 5:23); we will always have a body, soul, and spirit. Jesus who was the firstfruits of the resurrection (1 Corinthians 15:23), demonstrated to His disciples that He had a body and was not just a spirit (Luke 24:29). As physical beings, it is hard to get excited about an ethereal spirit world which has no relation to our current existence. But our eternal home will be on a New Earth (Revelation 21:1), a physical place that we will interact with in physical bodies.

Jesus ushering in the Eternal State does not mean the end of time. While God is outside the confines of time, we will not be. God created time to be a linear context for us physical creatures. This will not be suspended when we are resurrected. Time is just another dimension of our physical universe that we will also experience in eternity. In eternity, we will enjoy fruit from the tree of life that will help us measure the passage of time because it will yield twelve fruits in a year, a different one each month (Revelation 22:2).

People don't look forward to heaven because they expect it to be boring. But this is heretical thinking that says God is boring. It is a worldly perspective that considers sin to be exciting and righteousness to be dull. Drug addicts think they cannot be happy without their fix but this is the very source of their misery. Freedom from sin is freedom to fully experience the blessings God wants us to have.

Some people don't want to consider the soon return of Jesus because they fear their children will miss out on the joys of this life. But young people prematurely going to heaven will not miss out on a thing. Jesus said, *"I have come that they may have life, and that they may have it more abundantly"* (John 10:10). The abundant life is more than just quantity, an eternally long time; it is also characterized by wonderful quality beyond what we can even fully comprehend in our mortal condition (1 Corinthians 2:9).

People think heaven will be boring because they don't think there can be any challenges without sin. But just because we'll have a resurrected soul that doesn't cause us to be selfish doesn't mean we'll be perfect. We will be like Christ's human nature but we will not be Him and there will still be room for development. We will have deeper relationships to develop with God and our fellow creatures to His glory. And our learning will extend into eternity, *"that in the ages to come He might show the exceeding riches of His grace in His kindness toward us in Christ Jesus"* (Ephesians 2:7).

2.11 Looking Forward to Heaven

In heaven, we will each have an eternal body that will not grow old but this does not mean everyone will be equal and incapable of further improvement. Hard work will pay dividends even in heaven, *"My elect shall long enjoy the work of their hands"* (Isaiah 65:22).

We will not be idle in heaven, we will have gainful work to do as we reign with Christ over His creation (Revelation 5:10). God established a pattern of work and rest in the creation: *"on the seventh day God ended His work which He had done, and He rested on the seventh day"* (Genesis 2:2). And Jesus told us God never stopped working: *"My Father has been working until now, and I have been working"* (John 5:17). It was God's plan for people to work even before our fall into sin: *"Then the LORD God took the man and put him in the garden of Eden to tend and keep it"* (Genesis 2:15).

Work is only a burden in this world because of the consequences of sin: *"cursed is the ground for your sake; in toil you shall eat of it all the days of your life; both thorns and thistles it shall bring forth for you"* (Genesis 3:17-18). But during the Eternal State, *"there shall be no more curse"* (Revelation 22:3). Work has meaningful benefits beyond the paycheck even in this fallen world that is under the curse. Even now work is an outlet for our creativity that helps us build relationships. In eternity, we will more fully experience these benefits without the curse that often makes our work less than pleasant today.

In heaven, work will be exciting because the product of what we do will last forever. We will continually be learning and developing our skills so that our best work will always be ahead of us. We will forever enjoy the fruit of our labors because our minds and bodies will not degenerate. Worship of God is more than just praising God in song and listening to a sermon on Sunday mornings, it is everything we do to glorify God (Mark 12:30). We will worship God in our work, and there will be a lot of worship in heaven (Revelation 5:13).

There will be rewards for our service to God in this life (Luke 19:17). The better stewards we are of God's blessings, the greater capacity we'll have to participate in what God is doing in eternity. And consider Isaiah 9:7, *"of the increase of His government and peace there will be no end."* God is not done creating! We should want to be part of what He will be doing in eternity to the greatest extent possible.

God created the entire universe for us to explore. Jesus promised us, *"I will come again and receive you to Myself; that where I am, there you may be also"* (John 14:3). And He can go anywhere. Jesus demonstrated a capability of His resurrected body to materialize in a room full of His disciples (John 20:19). He did that intentionally to show us His resurrected body could make use of the spiritual domain to go anywhere in this physical universe. Our resurrected bodies will have that capacity and this will enable us to explore God's vast universe which would be impossible with our mortal physical constraints.

It is not just science fiction that we will be able to explore the stars. *"Now to Him who is able to do exceedingly abundantly above all that we ask or think, according to the power that works in us"* (Ephesians 3:20). Science fiction has an amazing propensity to eventually come to fruition. Our dream to explore the stars is the result of mankind's God-given sense of adventure, wonder, creativity, and imagination. As Randy Alcorn asked in his excellent book, "Heaven" - "Is God's imagination less than that of His image-bearers?" Visiting the stars will not only be possible in eternity, this will be one way we will come to know our Creator better by exploring His creation. *"Delight yourself also in the LORD, and He shall give you the desires of your heart"* (Psalm 37:4).

2.12 Being Heavenly Minded

Seek those things which are above, where Christ is, sitting at the right hand of God. Set your mind on things above, not on things on the earth (Colossians 3:1-2)

25

The more excited we get about heaven, the more we will want to study Bible prophecy and share the good news about it with others. It has been said that a person can be so heavenly minded, they are no earthly good. This sounds clever and some will think it may even be in the Bible but it is actually an unbiblical rationalization to be worldly. The Bible says the opposite; we should set our minds on heavenly things. The more we train our minds to see things from God's perspective, the better our decisions will be on the earth. The better we know and apply the principles behind the Law God has revealed to us, the better off we will be. When we face a choice, the best decision will be what is most honoring to God. The choices we make every day all have eternal ramifications. The better we can embrace God's eternal perspective, the more treasure we'll be able to lay up in heaven (Matthew 6:19-20).

3 END TIMES CHRONOLOGY

This chapter summarizes key end-times events as basic background for understanding Bible prophecy. The Tribulation and Rapture of the Church are described; and a thorough case is made for why we should expect a pre-Tribulation Rapture. The Millennial reign of Christ, the Eternal State, and hell are also summarized.

We are on the brink of some fantastic events associated with Jesus Christ's Second Advent. Everyone senses that dramatic change is in the air but only true born-again Christians who see the Bible literally as God's Word know what is about to happen. And God has told us what would happen with 100% accuracy. *"Remember the former things of old, for I am God, and there is no other; I am God, and there is none like Me, Declaring the end from the beginning, and from ancient times things that are not yet done, saying, 'My counsel shall stand, and I will do all My pleasure'* (Isaiah 46:9-10).

Many people have a problem taking the Bible literally because prophetic events are so incredible. But these scoffers conveniently ignore that God has poured out His wrath on earth before in the not-so-distant past (2 Peter 3:3-7). These people don't really know God as being Almighty enough to be outside the confines of time and thus accurately presenting and preserving His prophetic Word even using His error-prone creation.

The following is a summary of end time key events based on the most literal interpretation of Scripture. These summaries are chronological except for the Rapture of the Church which could happen at any time. The Tribulation is discussed first because a basic

27

understanding of this period of God's wrath helps us better appreciate why the Rapture of the Church must occur in advance of it.

3.1 The Tribulation

For then there will be great tribulation, such as has not been since the beginning of the world until this time, no, nor ever shall be (Matthew 24:21) Just prior to Jesus returning to establish His Millennial Kingdom, there will be a seven-year period of time when God pours out His wrath on the earth. He does this to prepare mankind for the 1,000-year reign of Christ on earth (Revelation 20:4). Most of the book of Revelation is about what happens during this terrible time. Jesus referred to an event in this seven-year period as the *"abomination of desolation"* (Matthew 24:15). This event happens in the middle of the seven-year Tribulation when the Antichrist comes into the future Jewish temple and declares himself to be God (Daniel 8:11, 9:27, 11:31; 2 Thessalonians 2:4). Jesus said that the *"abomination of desolation"* would begin what He called *"Great Tribulation"* (Matthew 24:21).

The complete seven-year period that includes the Great Tribulation is usually referred to as "The Tribulation" and starts when the Antichrist confirms a seven-year peace treaty with Israel (Daniel 9:27). In context, Daniel 9:27 has to refer to a week of years which is how we get the seven years; it makes no sense otherwise. The seven-year *"week"* of the Tribulation is preceded by 69 weeks of years starting with *"the command to build and restore Jerusalem"* and ending when *"Messiah shall be cut off"* (Daniel 9:25-26).

Daniel's 69 weeks of years or 483 years has happened in history. Nehemiah 2:1-8 says that Persian King Artaxerxes decreed that the wall of Jerusalem may be built in the twentieth year of his reign. From archeology we know Artaxerxes became king in 464 BC thus meaning the command to restore Jerusalem happened in 444 BC. Add the 483 years of the prophecy to 444 BC and we get 38 AD recognizing that there was no year "0". Allowing for the two to seven year error scholars say there was in beginning the Gregorian calendar, we get 31 to 36 AD, about the time Messiah Jesus would have been *"cut off"* by dying on the cross.

The Seventieth Week of Daniel is separated from the other 69 weeks of years because the Church Age would happen in between; a mystery during Old Testament times (Colossians 1:26-27). God was represented on earth by Israel during Daniel's 69 weeks of years followed by an interlude for an unspecified period of time where He has been working through the Church. But the Day is coming when the Church will be completed and there is one more week of years that He will resume working through Israel again, the Seventieth Week of Daniel which corresponds with the Tribulation and is called *"Jacob's trouble"* in Jeremiah 30:7.

3.2 Rapture of the Church

Jesus Christ's first advent demonstrated the immeasurable grace of God. He has been building and reigning over His Church Kingdom since He came to shed His blood for us on the cross (Colossians 1:13). But there will come a time when He will bring an end to the Church Age appearing to His own and call us into His presence at the Rapture of the Church. The Church began with the spectacular, supernatural indwelling of the Holy Spirit on Pentecost (Acts 2:1-4). The Church will likewise end with another spectacular, supernatural event in the Rapture of all followers of Christ, both living and dead.

3.3 Caught Up

The Lord Himself will come down from heaven, with a loud command, with the voice of the archangel and with the trumpet call of God, and the dead in Christ will rise first. After that, we who are still alive and are left will be caught up together with them in the clouds to meet the Lord in the air.
(1 Thessalonians 4:16-17, NIV)

The term "Rapture" is derived from the Latin word for "caught up." At the Rapture, the dead in Christ will rise first then living Christians will be translated into immortal bodies. Everyone agrees this passage tells us that all Christians living and dead will be resurrected together. What Christians disagree about is the timing of the Rapture. Most professing Christians are amillennialists who believe the Rapture of the Church will occur at the end of the age of mortals just prior to the Eternal State. However, Christians who take a more literal view of Scripture expect the Rapture to occur prior to the 1,000-year Millennial Reign of Christ on earth.

3.4 The Mystery of the Rapture

I tell you a mystery: We will not all sleep, but we will all be changed— in a flash, in the twinkling of an eye, at the last trumpet. For the trumpet will sound, the dead will be raised imperishable, and we will be changed. For the perishable must clothe itself with the imperishable, and the mortal with immortality. (1 Corinthians 15:51-53, NIV)

There will be a generation of people who do not die but will be suddenly *"changed"* (resurrected) into their eternal bodies directly from their mortal bodies. God did not reveal this amazing event to mankind prior to establishing the Church thus keeping it a mystery. But the Church was blessed with progressive revelation in the New Testament so we now know about it and look forward to it.

The term *"sleep"* in this passage is a euphemism for death. The original Greek word *"koimao"* that was translated *"sleep"* here means to be deceased, physical death. When the Rapture occurs, some Christians will still be living in their mortal bodies. So there will be a generation of Christians who will not taste death but be translated from our mortal bodies to our eternal, resurrected bodies in an instant. The resurrection of the entire population of the Church both living and dead will occur in a moment, in the twinkling of an eye. This is faster than a blink; people left on earth after the Rapture will sure be doing some blinking!

At the Rapture, our mortal bodies which are subject to corruption and mortality will be translated to new immortal bodies that will be immune to corruption. We will no longer have a sin nature which causes us to suffer the consequences of sin. We will be sinless with completed sanctification in glorified bodies like Christ has right now; He was the firstfruits of the resurrection (1 Corinthians 15:23).

3.5 Babies and Children Raptured

For the unbelieving husband is sanctified by the wife, and the unbelieving wife is sanctified by the husband; otherwise your children would be unclean, but now they are holy. (1 Corinthians 7:14)

Many futurist Christians believe that all children below the age of accountability will be taken to heaven at the Rapture. But the age of accountability is a cultural concept that is not supported in Scripture. However, it is clear that the children of Christians will be taken in the Rapture per 1 Corinthians 7:14. God is sovereign and may indeed take children in the Rapture even if they don't have a Christian parent. It is guaranteed that the Lord will do what is right from His perspective, not man's.

3.6 Those Left Behind

They refused to love the truth and so be saved. For this reason God sends them a powerful delusion so that they will believe the lie
(2 Thessalonians 2:10-11, NIV)

At the moment following the Rapture, there will be no believers left on earth. Left behind will be unbelievers and all who were merely professing Christians who claimed to be followers of Jesus but didn't really have a personal relationship with Him (Matthew 7:21-23). Upon realizing the Rapture has occurred, many professing Christians and other unbelievers will realize their error, repent of their sin and genuinely invite Jesus into their lives. In God's grace many souls will be saved following the Rapture. However, this means that they will probably lose their lives as martyrs during the Tribulation. But it is much better to lose your physical life and go to heaven than to survive the Tribulation only to end up in the lake of fire.

For the naturalists who have no room for supernatural acts of God in their worldview, there will be some plausible explanation for the Rapture. The world is already being set up for one likely explanation that the Rapture was due to extraterrestrial technology. There has been enough UFO interest that many people already believe earth is being visited by extraterrestrials. What they don't realize is that fallen angels following Satan are conditioning mankind to accept them as aliens from some distant planet. The deception will likely be that malevolent space aliens removed the Christians as an attack on earth so all mankind must now work together globally to deal with this threat. This will give us yet another reason to have a global government. And there will likely be friendly aliens offering to help mankind. Another variation of this deception is that helpful aliens purged those holding back society. The conventional wisdom will be that it is the Luddite, fundamentalist Christians who are impeding progress toward the utopian culture our society needs.

It is also possible that the Rapture will occur in the midst of a nuclear war which would be a huge distraction. Perhaps the missing Christians will be seen as collateral damage from the use of nuclear weapons. If people will believe that a tsunami is due to global warming, they will buy any explanation for people disappearing at the Rapture. And, who will miss a few million Christians when millions more have died from a nuclear war?

3.7 Importance of Timing

While the timing of the Rapture is controversial, those who take the most literal interpretation of Scripture are in agreement. Conservative biblical scholars know the Rapture occurs prior to the Tribulation. This means that the return of Jesus is in two phases; first for the Church at the Rapture, and second with the Church to establish His Millennial Kingdom.

There are no prophetic events that have to precede the Rapture; it is imminent and can happen at any time without warning. One of the paradoxes of the Christian faith is that we must live as if the Lord is returning today and also have a plan to build knowing that He may not come back for some time. The Rapture is the next major prophetic event happening prior to the Tribulation which culminates in the second coming of Jesus to earth.

It is important to have a correct view of the timing of the Rapture in order to better understand other aspects of Bible prophecy. There are just fewer interpretive conflicts that have to be resolved in understanding that the Rapture happens prior to the Tribulation.

If Christians don't recognize a correct timing of the Rapture, they may think it is God's plan for them to go through the Tribulation. This would be a source of discouragement God doesn't want us to have (1 Thessalonians 4:18). Instead, God wants us to expect that the Rapture could occur at any time and live our lives accordingly. The doctrine of the imminent Rapture is strong medicine against procrastination in serving God.

A wrong view of the timing of the Rapture can also lead to dangerous doctrines. For example, those thinking they will be going through the Tribulation, will be inclined to stock up on food, ammunition, and other supplies. While it is prudent to have supplies on-hand to get through a calamity like an earthquake or hurricane, God doesn't want His people to be survivalists squandering their resources by hoarding many months or even years of supplies. This is clearly an unbiblical doctrine since it teaches people to depend on their own resources for deliverance rather than trust in the power of God.

Another false doctrine which comes from the idea that the Church will go through the Tribulation is that the church has replaced Israel in the promises of God. God is not done working through Israel per Romans 11:26. He will resume using Israel as His representatives on earth during the Tribulation when He raises up

144,000 servant-evangelists (Revelation 7:1-8). Replacement theology which teaches that the Church has replaced Israel in God's plan for mankind is devil-inspired to keep people from discerning prophetic truth and is one of the roots of anti-Semitism.

3.8 The Pre-Trib Rapture

Alternative premillennial views about the timing of the Rapture have it occurring some time during or at the end of the Tribulation. But these views put the Church in the dubious position of looking for the Antichrist rather than our Lord. The Tribulation has very clear periods of time associated with certain key events. If the return of the Lord for His Church were not imminent, it would be possible to have a pretty good idea when it will happen. And this is contrary to the instructions He gave us: *"you also be ready, for the Son of Man is coming at an hour you do not expect"* (Matthew 24:44).

Just prior to telling us to be ready for the *"Son of Man"* to come for us, Jesus described the Rapture in Matthew 24:40-41; *"Then two men will be in the field: one will be taken and the other left. Two women will be grinding at the mill: one will be taken and the other left."* We know this has to be referring to the Rapture of the Church since it will be business as usual, *"they were eating and drinking, marrying and giving in marriage"* per Matthew 24:38. During the Tribulation, it will hardly be business as usual. There will be too many distractions with all the calamities from God pouring out His wrath for people to carry on with life as we mostly know it in the Church Age.

The book of Revelation provides a lot of details about what happens when God pours out His wrath during the Tribulation. For the most part, Revelation is in chronological order since Jesus told the Apostle John to, *"write the things which you have seen, and the things which are, and the things which will take place after this"* (Revelation 1:19). Indeed, the letters to the seven churches in Revelation Chapters Two and Three amazingly parallel actual Church history. In the book of Revelation the church is only seen again in heaven after Chapter Three. And Revelation 4:1 is a clear reference to the Rapture where John is called up to heaven to see what happens during the Tribulation.

The Apostle Paul certainly understood the Rapture to be imminent even during his day because he included himself among those who might not face death: *"the dead in Christ will rise first. After that, **we who are still alive** and are left will be caught up together with them in the* *clouds to meet the Lord in the air"* (1 Thessalonians 4:16-17, NIV, emphasis added). And Paul went on to say the doctrine of the Rapture was intended to be encouraging (1Thessalonians 4:8). Believing that we have to die or face the Tribulation before we are resurrected is anything but encouraging.

The Pre-Tribulation Rapture is further supported by God's promise that the Church would not suffer His wrath. *"For God did not appoint us to suffer wrath but to receive salvation through our Lord Jesus Christ"* (1 Thessalonians 5:9, NIV). The context of this passage tells us the term "wrath" refers to the Tribulation. God will save the church from suffering through the time when He pours out his wrath on the earth during the Tribulation.

The book of Second Thessalonians was written to put the Thessalonians at ease that the persecution they were suffering was not the Tribulation. If they were in the Tribulation, this would have meant that they missed the Rapture since Paul had taught them that the Rapture precedes the seven-year period of God's wrath. In 2 Thessalonians 2:7-8 we learn that the Holy Spirit is restraining evil enough that the Antichrist can not come to power as long as the Church is on earth. The Antichrist is revealed to the world is when he confirms a seven-year peace treaty with Israel at the beginning of the Tribulation (Daniel 9:27). The Church will not be on earth to witness that event.

Jesus said the Rapture would happen before He returns to earth to establish His Millennial Kingdom when He promised, *"I will come back and take you to be with me that you also may be where I am"* (John 14:2-3, NIV). Jesus didn't say He was coming here to be with us where we are as would be the case if He had the Second Coming in mind. He said He was coming to take us to be with Him where He is, in heaven. Jesus also said, *"He who believes in Me, though he may die, he shall live. And whoever lives and believes in Me shall never die"* (John 11:25-26). Thus Jesus said that there would be some living when He returned that would never die. This promise certainly applies to people who become believers during the Tribulation and survive to the end but it is also applicable to people at the end of the Church Age.

The pre-Tribulation Rapture has been maligned as a recent interpretation that wasn't believed for most of church history. The implication is that pre-Trib advocates are reading something into Scripture that isn't there. Many of those attacking the pre-Trib doctrine also see literal interpretation as being too "fundamentalist" preferring to believe that the Bible has too many divergent interpretations to even be God's Word. But Scripture does teach that prophecy is subject to "progressive illumination" in Daniel 12:4 and Jeremiah 30:24. Thus as developments unfold, later generations are in a better position to understand God's prophetic Word than even the prophet who wrote the prophecy.

3.9 Two Phases of Return

First Century Jews missed the Messiah's first coming because they expected Him to deliver them from Rome. Likewise, amillennialist Christians today will be caught by surprise at the Rapture because they expect it to be in conjunction with His ushering in the Eternal State. Since amillennialists do not expect a literal Tribulation, they don't believe there are any signs to watch for and thus will not be watching for Jesus.

A literal reading of Scripture teaches us that Jesus will return in two phases, first for the Church at the Rapture, then with the Church at His Second Coming. Thinking these two events occur at the same time as amillennialists do produces great confusion in trying to understand God's prophetic Word. There are irreconcilable differences between the passages referring to the Rapture and the Second Coming. The following summarizes the critical differences:

Seeing Jesus: At the Rapture, only believers will see Jesus while all people on earth will see Him at the Second Coming; compare Hebrews 9:28 with Revelation 1:7.

Meeting Jesus: At the Rapture, believers will meet Jesus in the air but at His Second Coming, He will physically set foot on the earth; compare 1Thess 4:17 with Zechariah 14:4 or Acts 1:10-11.

Resurrection: At the Rapture, all believers are resurrected but at the Second Coming no one is resurrected; compare Colossians 3:4 or Hebrews 9:28 with Revelation 19:11-15.

The Church: At the Rapture, the Church goes to heaven but at the Second Coming the Church returns to earth with Jesus; compare John 14:3 with 1Thessalonians 3:13 or Jude 14.

Judgment: At the Rapture, believers' works are judged to reveal the rewards that have been earned through faithful service. At the Second Coming, the nations are judged based on how they treated God's people; compare 1 Peter 1:7, 1 Cor 3:13-15 and Matt 25:31-32.

Predictability: The Rapture is imminent; it can not be predicted while the Second Coming is tied to key events of the Tribulation. And many of the key events of the Tribulation have a specific number of days given between them; for example, compare 1 Thess 5:2 with Daniel 12:11-13.

Timing: The Rapture occurs before God pours out His wrath during the Tribulation while the Second Coming happens at the end of the Tribulation which is also the end of God pouring out His wrath; compare 1 Thess 5:2 to Daniel 12:11-13 or Revelation 3:10 with Revelation 19:11. God in His grace reveals in Scripture the timing of the Second Coming so that those who trust in Jesus during the Tribulation will have hope knowing their suffering is limited.

Scripture References: The Rapture is revealed in the New Testament but veiled in the Old Testament while the Second Coming is prophesied in both. Even though the Rapture was a mystery in Old Testament times, there are some passages that were clearly talking about it in light of New Testament revelation; for example Psalm 12:1-2 and Micah 7:1-2. Also, the catching up of Enoch was a clear type of the Rapture occurring prior to God pouring out His wrath in the flood of Noah's day, see Genesis 5:24 and Hebrews 11:5.

Satan: Passages about the Rapture of the Church make no reference to Satan while we see that Satan will be incarcerated at the Second Coming; compare 2 Thessalonians 2:7 to Revelation 20:1-3.

3.10 Wrath of God

Then I saw another sign in heaven, great and marvelous: seven angels having the seven last plagues, for in them the wrath of God is complete (Revelation 15:1)

Soon after the Rapture of the Church, the seven-year Tribulation begins. This is when God pours out His wrath on earth to prepare mankind for the return of Jesus to establish His Millennial Kingdom. As we see the stage being set for the terrible events of the Tribulation, we know that the Rapture which precedes it has to be near.

3.11 Psalm 83 and Ezekiel 38 Wars

Psalm 83 and Ezekiel 38-39 describes two different wars that happen in the time-frame of the Lord's return. The Psalm 83 war involves nations surrounding Israel who want to see Israel *"cut off from being a nation"* (Psalm 83:4); just what we see today in the Palestinian conflict. The Ezekiel 38 war involves nations not directly involved in the Psalm 83 war led by Russia who wants to *"take great plunder"* (Ezekiel 38:13). Neither one of these wars are necessarily part of the Tribulation so one or both could happen prior to the Rapture of the Church. Some have pointed out that the Ezekiel 38 war likely occurs just prior to the Tribulation because Israel uses the captured weapons as fuel for seven years in Ezekiel 39:9. The significance of the reference to the seven years is that it may line up with the seven year Tribulation.

3.12 Antichrist Comes to Power

Either the Psalm 83 or Ezekiel 38 wars occurring prior to the Tribulation could constitute a world crisis providing the Antichrist with an ideal opportunity to step in and solve the Middle East problem. He will be an emerging world ruler and will probably take credit for Israel's deliverance from her enemies. The Antichrist will come to power when a coalition of ten world rulers yield their sovereignty to him (Revelation 17:12-13). He will broker a seven-year peace treaty for Israel which will have to include permission to build a temple in Jerusalem (Daniel 9:27). This effectively starts the countdown clock for the physical return of Jesus Christ to the earth which will occur seven years later to the day (Revelation 12:6).

3.13 A Bad Three and a Half Years

The first half of the Tribulation will be a time of relative prosperity and peace for Israel but it will be a terrible time for the world at large. The Antichrist will focus on consolidating his power as world ruler and engaging in his hobby of persecuting those who chose to follow Christ causing over a fourth of the world's population to die from wars and their aftermath (Revelation 6). Revelation 6:12-17 indicates that nuclear weapons will likely be used in these wars. The collateral damage of the Tribulation wars cause a third of the earth's vegetation to be burned up, a third of the salt and fresh waters to be poisoned, and a great cloud of radioactive dust to cover a third of the earth killing another third of mankind (Revelation 8:9).

3.14 Great Tribulation

The middle of the Tribulation will be marked with the Antichrist stopping the Hebrew sacrifices in the Jerusalem temple and declaring himself God (Matthew 24:15, Daniel 9:27, 11:31, 11:36). This will officially begin the Antichrist's persecution of Jews and cause Israel to flee to the wilderness where they are supernaturally protected by the Lord (Revelation 12:14). God pours out His wrath on the earth in the form of painful sores, poisoning of all the water, great heat, darkness, more warfare, and a great worldwide earthquake (Revelation 16). Then Jesus Christ, the King of kings and Lord of lords returns to the earth in great glory accompanied by the armies of heaven (Revelation 19:11-16). The armies of the Antichrist are destroyed by Jesus at Armageddon (Revelation 19:17-21).

3.15 Meanwhile in Heaven

The Church will be in heaven with Jesus during all the Tribulation events on the earth. Immediately after the Rapture, believers will be judged for their works to determine degrees of eternal reward (2 Corinthians 5:10). Believers are not judged for their sins, this was settled at the cross (John 5:24, 2 Corinthians 5:21, Galatians 3:13, Isaiah 53:5-6). War breaks out in heaven at the mid-point of the Tribulation between God's angels led by Michael and the fallen angels led by Satan who end up being cast out of heaven to the earth (Revelation 12:7-12). There is a great supper to celebrate the marriage of Jesus with His Bride, the Church (Revelation 19:7-9). Then we'll saddle-up on white horses to accompany Jesus in the Battle of Armageddon (Revelation 19:14). We as resurrected Church Age saints will be part of the Lord's own Airborne Cavalry; All the Way!

3.16 Armageddon

I saw three evil spirits that looked like frogs; they came out of the mouth of the dragon, out of the mouth of the beast and out of the mouth of the false prophet. They are spirits of demons performing miraculous signs, and they go out to the kings of the whole world, to gather them for the battle on the great day of God Almighty (Revelation 16:13-14, NIV)

UFOs and Science Fiction have prepared people to expect us to soon discover that "we are not alone in the universe." Indeed, the day will come when mankind will make contact with extraterrestrials. In the period just prior to the Lord's return, there will likely be a visitation of "good" aliens who promise deliverance from the "bad" aliens who threaten the earth. The extraterrestrials deceptively befriending mankind will incite the nations to join together in the battle of Armageddon.

Fallen angels are extraterrestrial demons who seek to thwart God's plan for mankind by tempting people to oppose God. While angels are non-corporeal spirit beings, they can manifest themselves as having physical bodies; *"do not forget to entertain strangers, for by so doing some have unwittingly entertained angels"* (Hebrews 13:2). It is interesting that the demon spirits of Revelation 16:13 are described as looking like frogs. Recall the images of little green or gray men that are universally described by people claming to be visited by the occupants of UFOs; they all have big eyes and smooth, nose-less features with heads shaped like frogs. People on earth will also be anticipating an extraterrestrial visitation because they will see the Lord coming from heaven: *"At that time the sign of the Son of Man will appear in the sky, and all the nations of the earth will mourn. They will see the Son of Man coming on the clouds of the sky, with power and great glory"* (Matthew 24:30, NIV).

3.17 Millennial Reign of Jesus

Jesus will have Satan locked-up (Revelation 20:1-3) then establishes His kingdom on earth where He fulfills His promises to Israel making them the leading nation in the world (Isaiah 60-62). Jesus will rule for 1,000 years (Revelation 20:4) from Jerusalem (Isaiah 24:23, Zechariah 14:9). Resurrected saints from the Church Age will govern the nations as administrators under Christ (Daniel 7:27, 2 Timothy 2:12, Revelation 2:26-27, 5:10). The nations will for the first time experience peace on earth during the Millennial Reign of Christ (Isaiah 2:4, 11:9). All creation will be freed from the curse of man's sin and restored to its original beauty, balance, and peace (Romans 8:18-23).

However, with all the blessings of the Millennial Kingdom going for them, many of the descendants of the believers who survived Armageddon will exercise their free will to reject Jesus as their Savior and Lord (Isaiah 64:17-20). Thus one of the purposes of the Millennial Kingdom is to demonstrate to mankind that they can not use the Flip Wilson defense, "the devil made me do it." The Millennial Kingdom unbelievers will stage one more futile rebellion when Satan is set free at the end of the 1,000-year reign of Christ (Rev 20:7-10).

3.18 Eternal State

Following the end of the Millennial Kingdom, Jesus judges all who died in rebellion and unbelief throughout time at the Great White Throne judgment (Revelation 20:11-15). They too are given eternal bodies but are condemned to the lake of fire where they'll be in torment forever. God will renovate heaven and earth by fire (2 Peter 3:10, Revelation 21:1) and His faithful will live with Him in a spectacular New Jerusalem forever (Revelation 20:9-27). The Bible gives us enough to know about what we will be doing in eternity to help us see that we will certainly not be bored!

3.19 Lake of Fire

Bible skeptics often dismiss God's Word by asking, "How could a loving God condemn people to hell for eternity?" But God is not doing the condemnation; people who reject Him do it to themselves per John 3:18. God created us to have a personal relationship with Him; spending eternity separated from Him will be the worst part of hell.

Some Christians deal with the terribleness of hell by embracing the doctrine of annihilation. This teaching makes a spiritualized interpretation of "eternal punishment" saying that it means forever ceasing to exist after a limited period of punishment in the lake of fire. While the doctrine of annihilation is a disputable matter within the pale of orthodoxy, it has problems besides not taking Scripture literally. One aspect of being in the image of God (Genesis 1:27) is that all people will continue to exist into eternity; as God will live into eternity future, so will we. God originally created Adam and Eve to never die so as their descendants we share that original plan of God; the only question is where we will spend eternity. Another problem with the doctrine of annihilation is this: Why would there be a resurrection of the spiritually dead per John 5:29 if they will only cease to exist?

We believers shouldn't allow the doctrine of annihilation to take the pressure off us. We are surrounded by people on the broad way to eternal punishment and thus should do all we can to help them see the need to have Jesus in their life before it is too late.

4 BIRTH PANGS

This chapter introduces a critical principle for understanding the signs Jesus gave us to recognize the general time-frame of His return. This chapter is an exposition of key verses in the Olivet Discourse relating them to trends and developments regularly seen in the news. Among the topics discussed are wars, persecution, false prophets, wild weather, and growing fearfulness.

Matthew 24 and Luke 21 record our Lord's answer to the questions His disciples asked about when He would return. In these passages referred to as the Olivet Discourse, Jesus told us what to watch for in terms of signs. This means Jesus wants us to know the season of His return; Hebrews 10:25 says that we can see the Day the Lord returns approaching and 1 Thessalonians 5:4 says that believers are not in darkness that we will be surprised by His return.

The signs Jesus gave where mostly common events that have happened throughout history but what makes them signs were that they will increase in frequency and intensity: *"All these are the beginning of sorrows"* (Matthew 24:8). The Greek word translated into *"sorrows"* is *"odin"* which means birth pains. The Tribulation will be a period of intense birth pains that culminates in the birth itself: the return of Jesus to restore order and set up His kingdom on earth. As we see events that will occur during the Tribulation happening with greater intensity and frequency, we know that the Tribulation will be coming soon. That is why it is important to keep an eye on world-wide developments.

As we observe various trends that set the stage for the intense events of the Tribulation, it becomes apparent that things can not keep going like this before there are serious consequences. Humanists will disregard these trends thinking that luck will intervene and mankind will prevail over these adverse trends; they think, *"all things continue as they were from the beginning"* (2 Peter 3:4). But a wise realist *"foresees evil and hides himself"* while *"the simple pass on and are punished"* (Proverbs 22:3). God is allowing birth-pangs to wake up the spiritually discerning to the nearness of the Tribulation.

What trend-ignoring humanists fail to consider is the exponential increase of developments common in nature. For example, the rate of bacteria growth in a culture is faster at the end of it's saturation than at the beginning. Developments foreshadowing the Tribulation will likewise grow exponentially; *"the end of it shall be with a flood"* (Daniel 9:26). Those not watching for the return of the Lord will be overwhelmed by events; they will be caught by surprise: *"For you yourselves know perfectly that the day of the Lord so comes as a thief in the night. For when they say, "Peace and safety!" then sudden destruction comes upon them, as labor pains upon a pregnant woman"* (1 Thessolonians 5:2-3).

The following are some birth pangs that are increasingly in the news:

4.1 Growing Messianic Deception

Many will come in My name, saying, 'I am the Christ,' and will deceive many (Matthew 24:4-5)

During the Tribulation, many will claim to be Jesus Christ. We have always had cult leaders but the number and impact of these deceivers will increase as we get closer to the Tribulation. The growth of "New Age" spirituality may be included here as well because of the claim that "you can be your own Christ." We might also include secular humanists who build up government to be mankind's provider and deliverer through socialism. Any person or institution considered to be mankind's Savior is the spirit of Antichrist and part of the Satan-inspired deception.

4.2 Wars, Rumors of Wars

You will hear of wars and rumors of wars. See that you are not troubled; for all these things must come to pass, but the end is not yet (Matthew 24:6)

The Tribulation will be characterized by war. We have always had wars but these will increase in frequency and intensity leading up to the Tribulation. More people were killed due to the wars of the Twentieth Century than all of human history. There have been plenty of wars in the 21st Century though with not nearly the carnage of the World Wars (but the Century is still young).

There have also been a lot of rumors of wars. This certainly includes hearing about war in a far place that doesn't directly affect us. All people in the U.S. during World War II were touched by the war even if they didn't lose a loved one because there was rationing and many businesses re-tooled to produce weapons and war supplies. Now it is a lot easier to ignore wars in far off places because they don't impact the worldwide economy nearly as much.

Another rumor of war is the threat of war like the "Cold War." This war involved those in the military but had very little impact on anyone else. We might also include the wars on poverty, drugs and terrorism as rumors of war. We have been fighting these wars for a long time with no apparent progress.

4.3 Racism

For nation will rise against nation (Matthew 24:7)
The Greek word translated *"nation"* in this passage is *"ethnos"* which refers to different ethnic people groups. So we can expect to see more instances of racism and genocide the closer we get to the Tribulation.

4.4 National Strife

Kingdom against kingdom (Matthew 24:7)
You'd think in this post Cold War era where everyone wants peace in the world that we wouldn't have any more conflicts between nations. But the perceived lower potential for nuclear war has seemingly given the green light to nations to go to war. People don't appear to be at a loss for finding reasons to justify wars; religion, trade, racism, political ideology, power, and all the other traditional reasons nations have ever gone to war are still motivations today. As the United Nations was started in the wake of World War II in an attempt to avoid more war, people will be ready to embrace the idea of a global government since peace continues to be so elusive.

4.5 Food Shortages

And there will be famines ...in various places (Matthew 24:7)

One of the unseen killers of warfare is famines that result from disrupting food production and distribution. So more wars mean more famines; and we still have the more traditional source of famine, bad weather. You'd think in this age of modern technology that food production would not be disrupted by the weather, but it still is. This problem is mitigated to some extent by global trade to take up the slack but since we are in the days leading up to the Tribulation when even bad weather is on the increase, we can expect to see more famines from multiple causes.

4.6 Pestilence

Pestilences ...in various places (Matthew 24:7)

You'd think that modern antibiotics would deliver us from most of the plagues that afflict people. But these do nothing for viruses and more bacterial infection strains are becoming resistant to antibiotics. Our dependence on global travel has made it increasingly difficult to contain outbreaks. There will be an increasing incidence of epidemics foreshadowing the Tribulation when terrible diseases will abound: *"They blasphemed the God of heaven because of their pains and their sores, and did not repent of their deeds"* (Revelation 16:11)

4.7 Beasts Attacking People

Power was given to them over a fourth of the earth, to kill...
by the beasts of the earth (Revelation 6:8)

The coming of the fourth horse of the Apocalypse will not only employ microscopic organisms to kill people but larger animals will turn against mankind as well. As we get closer to the Tribulation we can expect an increasing incidence of animals attacking people foreshadowing that terrible time when a fourth of earth's population is killed by wars, famine, pestilences, and other beasts. And this will likely occur during the first half of the Tribulation, another third of earth's population will die during the second half of the Tribulation, see Revelation 9:15.

4.8 Earthquakes

And earthquakes in various places (Matthew 24:7)

It is clear to everyone who is watching that earthquakes, volcanoes and tsunamis are increasing worldwide. Places that are not considered to be earthquake-prone are getting earthquakes. Some are blaming these on the hydraulic fracturing techniques that are being used in the U.S. to extract more oil from old oilfields. But that can not explain all the occurrences of earthquake swarms in places far from any fracking. This is an obvious sign to the spiritually discerning and just as you'd expect if we are getting close to the end of the Age.

4.9 Persecution

Then they will deliver you up to tribulation and kill you, and you will be hated by all nations for My name's sake. (Matthew 24:9)

Persecution of "infidels" has become so pervasive in Islamic countries that some areas no longer have any Christians at all. We have been blessed in the United States that persecution of Christians is significantly more subtle. But we can already see by the increasing rate Christians are marginalized in the media that persecution will come to this country as well. What a person thinks of homosexual behavior has become a litmus test for whether they are on-board with society moving forward or not. Marginalization will eventually lead to outright persecution of Christians because we'll be seen as holding society back. The Scriptural claims of exclusivity for going to heaven such as John 14:6 simply can not be tolerated by the hypocritical cultural elite who say it is the Christians who are intolerant. However, it will be much better to be a follower of Christ during this current Church Age than to become one during the Tribulation.

4.10 Betrayal

And then many will be offended, will betray one another, and will hate one another. (Matthew 24:10)

Ever notice how liberals are so easily offended by something they deem to be politically incorrect? It is hard to believe that they are really offended; they are just using that as an excuse to advance an agenda. And loyalty is cheap in this postmodern age of changing conditional morality. People in this age will drop their friends for the most trivial of reasons even stirring up hatred which is so easily done as the love grows cold (Matthew 24:12).

4.11 False Prophets

Then many false prophets will rise up and deceive many (Matthew 24:11)
There seems to be an increasing number of experts who claim to speak for God today. As the trends of this world become more obviously disturbing, there will be many more who say they have the answer. But God has already given us the answers in His Word. People who do not know God's Word, are easily fooled by false prophets. The best way to avoid being *"carried about with every wind of doctrine"* (Ephesians 4:14) is to be well grounded in God's Word. *"For the Word of God is living and powerful... and is a discerner of the thoughts and intents of the heart"* (Hebrews 4:12).

4.12 Lawlessness, Lack of Love

And because lawlessness will abound, the love of many will grow cold (Matthew 24:12)
Fewer and fewer people in this Age understand the agape love of Christ. The conventional wisdom is that love is an emotion, a feeling that can come or go. This is a very selfish notion of love but it is the best the world can offer. And we wonder why relationships just don't last in this day. True godly love is not a feeling; it is an act of the will. It is the sacrificial love that Jesus demonstrated on the cross. As people turn away from God, they turn away from His Love that is only possible in people who know Him (Galatians 5:22).

4.13 Gospel Preached Worldwide

This gospel of the kingdom will be preached in all the world as a witness to all the nations, and then the end will come (Matthew 24:14)
During the Tribulation there will be no excuse for not knowing the good news about Jesus Christ. God will supernaturally announce it to the world: *"Then I saw another angel flying in the midst of heaven, having the everlasting gospel to preach to those who dwell on the earth-- to every nation, tribe, tongue, and people"* (Revelation 14:6). We certainly have a foreshadowing of this today with radio, television, and the Internet making it easy to find the good news of Jesus. And exposure to the gospel is especially easy in America where churches abound. Certainly not all people have as easy access as we do in the U.S. but during the Tribulation it will be hard to ignore that God is at work and time is running out for people to allow Him into their lives.

4.14 Great Tribulation

For then there will be great tribulation, such as has not been since the
beginning of the world until this time, no, nor ever shall be (Matthew 24:21)

The seven-years of the Tribulation will be bad, but the second half of
this period will be the worst. God in His grace gives us plenty of
warning for this terrible period of history. There are more prophecies
in Scripture of the Tribulation then any other future event. Jesus gave
us the birth pang signs to show us when we are nearing the Tribulation. Even during the Tribulation God's warning to mankind will be
hard to ignore because the fulfillment of Bible prophecy will be characterized by escalating severity.

4.15 Wholesale Death

And unless those days were shortened, no flesh would be saved;
but for the elect's sake those days will be shortened (Matthew 24:22)

There will be a lot of dying during the Tribulation. Over half the
population of earth will die per Revelation 6:8 and 9:18. It is hard to
imagine such carnage before the advent of nuclear weapons. It is
likely that such weapons of mass destruction will be used during the
Tribulation; God wouldn't have allowed mankind to develop such
terrible weapons if He did not have a purpose for them.

4.16 Mass Animal Deaths

The land will mourn; and everyone who dwells there will waste away
with the beasts of the field and the birds of the air; even the fish
of the sea will be taken away. (Hosea 4:3)

It will not just be people who suffer during the Tribulation; animals
will die off in mass as well. It is interesting that birds and fish are
specifically mentioned here and again in Zephaniah 1:3. There have
been increasing instances of mysterious die-offs of birds and fish. We
can expect more as we get closer to the Tribulation.

4.17 Signs and Wonders

For false christs and false prophets will rise and show great signs
and wonders to deceive, if possible, even the elect (Matthew 24:24)

Not only will there be a lot of false prophets claiming to speak for
God during the Tribulation, there will also be some claiming to be
Christ. You would expect that as the spirit of Antichrist grows. It is
likely the *"other beast"* of Revelation 13:11 who will cause people to

worship the Antichrist will be the False Prophet who claims to be Christ. Certainly the Muslims are expecting Jesus to return to convince Christians to worship their messiah, al-Mahdi.

The Tribulation religious leaders will be very convincing because they will be able to perform great supernatural-appearing feats. They will have a lot of help performing these deceptions because Satan's complete cadre of fallen angels will be on earth having been banished from the spiritual realm per Revelation 12:4-12.

4.18 Astronomical Events

There will be signs in the sun, in the moon, and in the stars (Luke 21:25)
The greatest astronomical event ever will be when Jesus Christ returns; *"Behold, He is coming with clouds, and every eye will see Him"* (Revelation 1:7). But there will be other signs in the heavens that foreshadow His return; *"the sun became black as sackcloth of hair, and the moon became like blood"* (Revelation 6:12, see also Joel 2:31). So we can expect other spectacular developments in the heavens as birth pangs the closer we get to the Tribulation. These developments should serve to shake up the uniformitarians who believe, *"all things continue as they were from the beginning"* (2 Peter 3:4). But they are unfortunately so blinded by their religion of naturalism that they'll dismiss these signs as mere coincidences.

4.19 Wild Weather

On the earth distress of nations, with perplexity, the sea and the waves roaring (Luke 21:25)
Jesus is sending the spiritually discerning a message about the closeness of His return in the increasing instances of record setting weather events we have been experiencing. This is also making it easy to sell people on the idea that global warming is really happening. Clearly anyone can see that something is up and the global warming lobby takes full advantage of it. The global visionary deceivers have even re-branded "global warming" as "climate change" to be able to use it to explain record cold weather as well. People with the climate change religion are rabid about the need to do something now. Their onerous requirements to cut back carbon dioxide emissions have no bounds, even if it harms people in the process. What they do not realize is that they are the "useful idiots" of those who want to see governmental power centralized globally.

4.20 Growing Fear

Men's hearts failing them from fear and the expectation of those things which are coming on the earth, for the powers of heaven will be shaken.
(Luke 21:26)

Anyone who bothers to consider the trajectory of the many trends we are seeing in the world today would have to conclude that we are rapidly heading toward a culmination of history. The wild weather is one trend that has the global warming advocates fearful enough to take radical measures in an attempt to reverse it; as if that were possible. There will also be perplexing developments in the heavens that will be the source of more fear. Expect the growing turbulence among the nations to bring renewed fear of nuclear war. Nuclear weapons will be used in the Tribulation and maybe even before. The powers of heaven will be shaken with thermonuclear weapons that employ fusion, the same process going on in the sun and stars.

4.21 Israel Maturing

Now learn this parable from the fig tree: When its branch has already become tender and puts forth leaves, you know that summer is near
(Matthew 24:32)

The fig tree is a symbol of Israel (Hosea 9:10 and Joel 2:21-25). The generation that sees Israel preparing to bear fruit as a nation will be the generation that sees the return of Jesus (Matthew 24:34). The fig tree of Israel started sprouting leaves when it became a nation in 1948. There will be a generation of people who was alive when that happened who will see the return of Christ.

4.22 Days of Noah

As the days of Noah were, so also will the coming of the Son of Man be
(Matthew 24:37)

The signs given here are what characterized life in Noah's day: demon possession, wickedness, evil thoughts, corruption and violence (Genesis 6:4-13). So we can expect to see more of the evil of Noah's day as we get closer to the Rapture of the Church.

4.23 Imminent Rapture

Watch therefore, for you do not know what hour your Lord is coming
(Matthew 24:42)

Our Lord admonishes us to watch for Him because He could come for His Church at any time with virtually no warning. Any attempt to pick when the Rapture will occur is a futile exercise. People who have done that discredit the Bible when the day they determined for the Rapture comes and goes without it happening. God's purpose for the imminent Rapture is that we live our lives ready for it.

4.24 Seeing Birth Pangs in the News

Now when these things begin to happen, look up and lift up your heads, because your redemption draws near (Luke 21:28)

Jesus told us about the principle of the birth pangs to help us know when we are getting close to His return. As we see developments foreshadowing the Tribulation, we know we are even closer to the Rapture which precedes it. So when we recognize birth pangs in the news, we can be encouraged that this only brings us that much closer to the Day Jesus comes for His Church and we will receive our glorified, resurrected bodies.

5 ISRAEL

Israel is the most important and obvious sign of the times. All Scripture is from Israel's perspective and every day there are news reports showing how prophecies of the nation of Israel have been fulfilled or the stage is being set for them to be realized. Many prophecies were fulfilled in developments related to Israel becoming a nation and there are aspects of the peace process which are prophetic along with the growth of anti-Semitism world-wide.

Fredric II, King of Prussia (1740-1786) asked Joachim von Zieten, General of the Hussars, a Christian known to be well grounded in his faith to, "Give me proof for the truth of the Bible in two words!" General von Zeiten replied, "Your majesty, the Jews!" Indeed God has blessed and preserved the nation of Israel as no other nation on earth.

God has used the Jews to represent Himself to humanity. All of the Bible was written by Jews under the inspiration of the Holy Spirit. The Lord Jesus Christ was born a Jew. God is not done using the Jews; there are promises He made to Israel that are yet to be fulfilled.

The most prolific prophecy in the Old Testament is about Israel returning to the land prior to Jesus coming back to establish His Millennial Kingdom. Preterits claim all the prophecies about the Jews returning to the land have been fulfilled in history by the Jews returning from captivity in Babylon. But the context and a literal reading of these texts make it clear that most of these prophecies actually refer to the time just preceding the return of Christ.

The following are prophetic topics that often come up in the news regarding Israel and the Jews:

5.1 Uniqueness of the Jews

The LORD has proclaimed you to be His special people.
(Deuteronomy 26:18)

The Lord ordained that the Jews would be a special people, unique in all the world. God revealed Himself to us through the Hebrew prophets, disciples and Jesus Christ. It is clear that God has a special place in His heart for Jews blessing them with greater achievements than any other people groups. Jews are leaders in all fields; a higher percentage of Nobel prizes have gone to Jews than any other race of people. Jews tend to be wealthier than their peers which has stirred up jealousies rising to anti-Semitism.

5.2 Protection of the Jews

He who touches you touches the apple of His eye (Zechariah 2:8)

God has chosen the Jewish nation to reveal Himself through and thus be a blessing to all people (Genesis 12:2). So when people mess with God's chosen vessel Israel, they are really messing with the Almighty. While God has used nations to punish Israel for their infidelity to Him, He has always preserved a remnant of faithful followers.

5.3 Preservation of Jewish Cultural Identity

For I am the LORD, I do not change; therefore you are not consumed,
O sons of Jacob. (Malachi 3:6)

The uniqueness of the Jews has been preserved despite the Diaspora, the worldwide dispersion of the Jews that happened soon after the Romans sacked Jerusalem in 70AD. While most Jews today are not religious, they have maintained their cultural heritage wherever they have gone. The Jews not being assimilated into local cultures for multiple centuries is unprecedented in history.

5.4 Revival of the Jews

For I do not desire, brethren, that you should be ignorant of this mystery, lest
you should be wise in your own opinion, that blindness in part has happened
to Israel until the fullness of the Gentiles has come in. (Romans 11:25)

God has made separate promises to Israel and the Church and He is not done working through Israel as a nation. The role of the Jews did not end with the founding of the Church, it was suspended until the Church is completed. The Church Age will end at the Rapture and God will again work through the Jews.

5.5 Return of the Jews

For I will take you from among the nations, gather you out of all countries, and bring you into your own land. (Ezekiel 36:24)

This prophecy of the return of the Jews refers to a re-gathering from multiple nations; it can not refer to a return from captivity of the single nation of Babylon. The context here makes it clear that the Jews are returning to the land of Israel in unbelief. This is exactly what has been occurring; Israel is essentially a secular nation in the model of Europe and the United States.

5.6 Return of the Jews is Permanent

Then they shall dwell in the land that I have given to Jacob My servant, where your fathers dwelt; and they shall dwell there, they, their children, and their children's children, forever (Ezekiel 37:25)

Once the Jews return to the land from all the nations in the world, they are there from now on. God will not allow all the threats to their existence to uproot them from the land of Israel. Why would an Omnipotent God who is in control allow Israel to again be uprooted from the land He gave them before they have had an opportunity to fulfill His purpose for them? It is not God's pattern to prematurely end restoration before they turn back to Him. The Jews are in Israel to stay, see also Amos 9:14-15.

Ezekiel 37:24 and 25b tells us that King David will again rule over over Israel. Taken literally, this can only refer to a resurrected King David during the Millennial Kingdom. The millennial reign of Christ will have resurrected saints serving in positions of authority in the Lord's government.

Ezekiel 37:22 reveals that Israel will no longer be a divided country as they were in the days of their kings. This is certainly the case today. While the Jews return to Israel in unbelief, Ezekiel 37:23 makes it clear that God will restore their national relationship to Him; the nation of Israel will return to being God's people following the Rapture of the Church.

5.7 Restoration of Israel to God

*And I heard the number of those who were sealed. One hundred and
forty-four thousand of all the tribes of the children of Israel were sealed*
(Revelation 7:4)

The Jews as a nation will return to being God's people during the
Tribulation as represented by 144,000 or 12,000 from each of the 12
tribes who go out preaching that Jesus is the Messiah. This is God
working through the nation of Israel again to help people to know
Him. A great multitude of people will respond to these Jewish evangelists because supernatural fulfillment of prophecy will be a regular
occurrence during the Tribulation.

5.8 Restoration of the Land of Israel

*The wilderness and the wasteland shall be glad for them, and the desert
shall rejoice and blossom as the rose* (Isaiah 35:1)

Mark Twain visited the land of Israel in 1867 and published what he
saw in his book, "Innocents Abroad." He described the land as being a barren wasteland, devoid of both vegetation and human population. All that has changed with the Jews returning to the land. God
has made the desert bloom increasing the rainfall over 450% since
1900. And He has even restored the forests with over 400 million
trees since the Jews have returned to the land.

*Those who come He shall cause to take root in Jacob; Israel shall blossom
and bud, and fill the face of the world with fruit.* (Isaiah 27:6)

Today, Israel is one of the few nations on earth that exports more
food than it imports. God has blessed Israel with technology enabling
them to make good use of the water they have pioneering innovative
irrigation in their arid land; see also Amos 9:13.

5.9 Order of Jews Returning

*Fear not, for I am with you; I will bring your descendants from the east, and
gather you from the west; I will say to the north, 'Give them up!' And to the
south, 'Do not keep them back!' Bring My sons from afar, and My daughters
from the ends of the earth* (Isaiah 43:5-6)

When biblical prophecy is fulfilled, it is exact in every detail. Even the
order of the Jews returning to the land of Israel was prophesied.
Their return began in the Middle East from Syria, Iraq, and Jordan in
1930-1940. Then the Jews returned from Western Europe after

WWII due to the holocaust. They returned from Russia which is north of Israel starting in 1988 and finally from Ethiopia to the south as part of Operation Solomon, in the summer of 1991. The Jews are officially back in their land!

5.10 Restoration of the Hebrew Language

For then I will restore to the peoples a pure language (Zephaniah 3:9)

A pure language that was lost will be restored in the end times; Hebrew is the only language lost for everyday use that has ever been restored. There are fewer languages in the world than there once were and some have been effectively lost as a commonly spoken language like Latin. Languages and dialects are consolidating as the world seeks to work together more thus attempting to reverse what happened at the Tower of Babel.

During the dispersion of Israel, Hebrew as a spoken language was all but lost; only biblical scholars could read it. The Hebrew language was corrupted with others; Ladino was an amalgamation of Hebrew and Spanish, Yiddish combined Hebrew with German. Eliezer Ben-Yehuda dedicated his life to reviving the pure Hebrew language inventing thousands of new words needed by modern society based on Hebrew root words. Today Hebrew is the language that binds Israelis together despite their coming from different nations. Israelis can now read original biblical scrolls without translation. You can't say the same thing about English; Old English is almost unintelligible to us today.

Bible skeptics say the restoration of the Hebrew language was self-fulfilling prophecy. But why would a secular people feel the need to fulfill Bible prophecy just to prove it to be true? It would have been much easier for the Jews to consolidate their nation around a language that was already in use. English is the worldwide language of commerce, science and technology. It would have been a whole lot less trouble to just use English rather than resurrect and update Hebrew, but God ordained that Hebrew would be spoken in Israel when the Jews returned. This is powerful evidence that God is not done with Israel.

5.11 Restoration of Jerusalem

*They will fall by the sword and will be taken as prisoners to all the nations.
Jerusalem will be trampled on by the Gentiles until the times of the Gentiles
are fulfilled.* (Luke 21:24, NIV)

The fulfillment of this prophecy has been foreshadowed by Israel re-
taking possession of Jerusalem as part of the Six-Day War in 1967 for
the first time since they were dispersed by the Romans in 70 A.D.
Since 70 A.D., Jerusalem has been under the governments of the
Romans, Byzantines, Arabs, Crusaders, Mamlukes, Turks, British,
and Jordanians. Israel is in control of Jerusalem today but they allowed the Islamists to retain control of the Temple Mount. So the
heart of Jerusalem is still being trampled on by Gentiles but that day
will end by the return of the Messiah. Israel will control the Temple
Mount during the Tribulation because they have to build a Jewish
temple there in order for the *"abomination of desolation"* to take place
(Matthew 24:15, Daniel 8:11, 9:27, 11:31, 2 Thessalonians 2:4).

5.12 Restoration of a Temple in Jerusalem

*Forces shall be mustered by him, and they shall defile the sanctuary fortress;
then they shall take away the daily sacrifices, and place there the
abomination of desolation.* (Daniel 11:31)

There has to be a Jewish temple in Jerusalem at the mid-point of the
Tribulation in order for the abomination of desolation to take place
as Jesus referred to in Matthew 24:15-16. This looks impossible today
with an Islamic mosque on the Temple Mount. Muslims consider
Jerusalem to be their third holiest site which is surprising since Jerusalem is not even mentioned in the Quran. But God said there would
be a third temple in Jerusalem so there will be. Indeed, there is today
a lot of interest in Israel for a temple because it is seen as being a key
part of Israel's national identity.

5.13 Jerusalem in the News

*It shall happen in that day that I will make Jerusalem a very heavy stone
for all peoples; all who would heave it away will surely be cut in pieces,
though all nations of the earth are gathered against it.* (Zechariah 12:3)

Ever wonder why there is always something about Jerusalem in the
news? Jerusalem is the hardest nut to crack in the pursuit of world
peace. So the peace of Jerusalem stands in the way of world peace. If

we can resolve the conflict over Jerusalem then there is no conflict in the world that we cannot resolve.

Eventually all nations will oppose Israel. This has already begun with most of the United Nations resolutions being in opposition to Israel. But the nations that become an enemy of Israel are really setting themselves up to be an enemy of God which has severe consequences; *"For thus says the LORD of hosts: 'He sent Me after glory, to the nations which plunder you; for he who touches you touches the apple of His eye'"* (Zechariah 2:8).

5.14 Israel's Beginning

Before she was in labor, she gave birth; before her pain came, she delivered a male child. Who has heard such a thing? Who has seen such things? Shall the earth be made to give birth in one day? Or shall a nation be born at once? For as soon as Zion was in labor, she gave birth to her children. (Isaiah 66:7-8)

Israel was born as a nation in a single day on May 14, 1948 then immediately was plunged into a war with her Arab neighbors. Most nations form following war, but with Israel it was the other way around. The day following the establishment of a Jewish state in the land of Israel, the armies of four Arab countries, Egypt, Syria, Transjordan and Iraq, entered what had been British Mandatory Palestine launching the 1948 Arab–Israeli War. Saudi Arabia sent a military contingent to operate under Egyptian command and Yemen declared war but did not take military action. The fact that Israel survived this war against overwhelming odds was a miracle and proof of deliverance from God.

5.15 Israel's Flag

*And in that day there shall be a Root of Jesse, who shall stand
as a banner to the people* (Isaiah 11:10)

The flag of Israel uses the Star of David and King David was a son of Jesse, thus the root of Jesse. There are a lot of other symbols they could have chosen for their flag. The emblem of Israel is an Escutcheon which contains a Menorah in its center, two olive branches on both sides of the Menorah and the label "Israel" in Hebrew at the bottom. But they chose a star of David for their flag. Is this self-fulfilling prophecy or God declaring the end from the beginning? It is hard to swallow the idea that a secular nation chose a symbol just to say they have fulfilled Bible prophecy.

5.16 Israel is Israel

Thus says the Lord GOD: "Behold, O My people, I will open your graves and cause you to come up from your graves, and bring you into the land of Israel." (Ezekiel 37:12)

It is significant that the land of Israel will be called Israel when the Jews return. The land of Israel could have been called Palestine, Galilee, Samaria, or Judah but it now known by its biblical name, Israel.

5.17 Democracy in the Middle East

The governors of Judah shall say in their heart, "The inhabitants of Jerusalem are my strength in the LORD of hosts, their God." (Zechariah 12:5)

The end times government of Israel will differ from ancient times. They will have governors rather than kings. Israel will be ruled by a democracy rather than a monarchy. Indeed, they are the only truly functioning democracy in the Middle East. Some of the nations around Israel have tried but they just can't make it work. Also note here that the leaders of Israel during this time will be secular because they refer to the Lord as *"their God"* rather than "our God."

5.18 Israel's Military Prowess

In that day I will make the governors of Judah like a firepan in the woodpile, and like a fiery torch in the sheaves; they shall devour all the surrounding peoples on the right hand and on the left. (Zechariah 12:6)

Israeli forces have won against superior forces in 1948, 1956, 1967, 1973, and 1981. Today the Israeli Defense Force is the most powerful in the region and Israel is currently the only nation in the Middle East with nuclear weapons. God has protected Israel from its inception and has enabled them to build a military capability that has brought them security and stability.

5.19 Israel's Political Prowess (Zechariah 12:6)

Prime Minister Netanyahu is the only leader in the Middle East who speaks the truth about the threat of Islamic terrorism to Western Civilization. His speaking truth and common sense resonates much louder than the spin-doctored propaganda serving a politically correct agenda that comes from most politicians in the West. But the world doesn't want Truth so we will have Tribulation.

5.20 Israel's Enemies

They have said, "Come, and let us cut them off from being a nation,
that the name of Israel may be remembered no more." (Psalm 83:4)

The stage is being set for Israel to devour the enemies who surround them. Most of the Middle East Muslim nations want to push Israel into the sea and are preparing for war. Every previous attack made on Israel has resulted in Israel taking more land. The next war will likely do the same thing and resolve the Palestinian problem once and for all.

5.21 Land for Peace

I will also gather all nations, and bring them down to the Valley of
Jehoshaphat; and I will enter into judgment with them there on account
of My people, My heritage Israel, whom they have scattered among the
nations; they have also divided up My land. (Joel 3:2)

God does not like the peace process imposed on Israel where they are expected to give up land for peace. Israel's enemies do not even recognize their right to exist and will not be happy until the State of Israel ceases to exist. God is the one who originally gave Israel their land and will make sure that all of it will be restored to them. Those opposing the will of God will suffer His wrath.

5.22 Spirit of Antichrist in Peace Process

He shall… divide the land for gain (Daniel 11:39)

The solution of the world to bring peace to Israel is to divide the land of Israel. The spirit of Antichrist is to oppose God and His plan. Those seeking to do that will have their day with devastating consequences during the Tribulation. We can already see this spirit of Antichrist in the world and it is getting more pervasive as we get closer to the Tribulation (1 John 4:3). Jesus said there would be birth pangs that foreshadow His coming (Matthew 24:8) and the spirit of Antichrist is among them.

5.23 Anti-Semitism

Alas! For that day is great, so that none is like it; and it is the time
of Jacob's trouble, but he shall be saved out of it. (Jeremiah 30:7)

As we get closer to the Tribulation, we can expect to see more instances of anti-Semitism. This is why many thought that the holocaust during World War II heralded the Tribulation. But it was just a birth pang and we can expect to see more anti-Semitism birth pangs. The world irrationally supports Palestinian terrorists who will not rest until Israel ceases to exist. You would think that the world would support Israel as a viable working democracy trying to defend itself but that is not what is happening. Terrorist murderers are praised for their valiant struggle in resisting while Israel is condemned for responding.

Anti-Semitism is an irrational demonic sickness where hatred of the Jew has become hatred of the Jewish State. How a person regards God has a direct bearing on how they regard God's people Israel. Those who hate the Jews and Israel have opened up their mind to the god of this world. Anti-Semitism is growing in the spirit of Antichrist.

5.24 Judgment for Israel's Enemies

I will bless those who bless you, and I will curse him who curses you; and in you all the families of the earth shall be blessed. (Genesis 12:3)

Going against the will of God in opposing Israel is not a good policy, it invites God's wrath. There will be consequences when nations try to force Israel into something that is not in their best interest.

6 SPIRIT OF ANTICHRIST

The Spirit of Antichrist is seen in daily news developments as the world trends further away from the God of the Bible. God is removing His restraint of evil as we get closer to the return of Jesus. God's plan and purpose for allowing evil is discussed in this chapter along with the characteristics of the man who will personify evil, the Antichrist.

Christianity used to be well regarded in the United States. Indeed, the freedom to worship Jesus Christ without government meddling motivated the first settlers and founding fathers of the United States. But increasingly there is an undercurrent of animosity against Christ and His followers in this country. It is the Christians who are seen as holding society back from where the culture is headed.

The growing animus toward Christians is accelerating as we get closer to the return of Jesus. At the same time, the spirit of Antichrist is growing; *"every spirit that does not confess that Jesus Christ has come in the flesh is not of God. And this is the spirit of the Antichrist, which you have heard was coming, and is now already in the world"* (1 John 4:3).

The spirit of Antichrist is not recognizing Jesus as the Son of God, our Savior and Lord. It is replacing Him with such things as deliverance from a government to take care of us, wealth, or anything else that makes it possible for people to think they can get by without Jesus in their lives.

6.1 Removing the Restraint of Evil (2 Thessalonians 2:1-10)
The Bible passage which best addresses the coming of the law-

less one as a result of the Holy Spirit removing His restraint of evil is 2 Thessalonians 2:1-10. This passage can only be properly understood from a premillennial perspective which takes the most literal interpretation of Scripture. Jesus returns in two phases, first for His followers at the Rapture of the Church and next at the end of the Tribulation to establish His promised Kingdom on earth.

When the Apostle Paul wrote his second letter to the Thessalonians, their persecution was so bad some of them thought they were in the Tribulation which would mean they missed the Rapture. Paul wrote to clarify why that was not the case and in the process helped us understand more about what happens leading up to the Antichrist's rise to power.

In verse 2:1, Paul made it clear he was elaborating on *"our gathering together to Him."* This can only refer to the Rapture of the Church that he told the Thessalonians about in his first letter to them (1 Thessalonians 4:13-18). Paul sought to reassure the Thessalonians that the Tribulation had not come yet in verse 2. The term *"day of Christ"* was understood to refer to the Tribulation because it culminates in the revelation of Christ to the world.

In verse 2:3, Paul said that the Tribulation *("that Day")* would not come until two things happen: (1) the *"falling away"* and (2) the *"man of sin is revealed."* The *"falling away"* either refers to an apostasy which is a falling away from the faith or a falling away of believers from the earth. Either way, the removal of the Church at the Rapture is implied here because the Rapture results in zero believers on earth; as thorough a falling away of the faith as there could possibly be.

In verse 2:3, the *"man of sin"* is also called *"the son of perdition"* and later, *"the lawless one"* in verse 8. Given this coupled with the fact that he *"opposes and exalts himself above all that is called God or that is worshiped"* (verse 4), he can only be the Antichrist. This person will likely be a man possessed by Satan as Judas was at the time of Christ (John 13:27). Thus, the Antichrist can not come on the scene until the Church is removed at the Rapture. This is why any efforts to anticipate who the Antichrist is would be a futile waste of time.

In verse 2:4, we learn that the Antichrist will represent himself as God in the temple. This means that during the Tribulation there will have to be a Jewish temple in Jerusalem. Thus the current political situation in the Middle East must change to allow a Jewish temple to be built there. Jesus called the event where the Antichrist will represent himself as God in the temple as the *"abomination of desolation"* in Matthew 24:15 referring to Daniel 8:11-14, 9:27, 11:31, and 12:11. This *"abomination of desolation"* is the point at which the Jews as a nation realize that the world leader is not their Savior but a deceiver. Jesus warns them that they better flee Jerusalem at that point because serious persecution will follow it (Matthew 24:16-20).

In verses 2:6-7 we learn that *"He who now restrains lawlessness is already at work"* keeping evil at bay and the Antichrist from emerging. The Holy Spirit in the role of the Restrainer is keeping the Antichrist from coming to power while the Church is on earth. The *"mystery of lawlessness"* is that Satan and his minions are conspiring to thwart God's plans to call out a people for Himself. Jesus revealed this in His parable of the wheat and tares, Matthew 13. The time will come when the Restrainer will be taken out of the way. The Holy Spirit who is currently restraining evil will abruptly end this ministry when the Church is taken out of the world at the Rapture. As we see evil growing worse per 2 Timothy 3:13, we recognize this as foreshadowing the complete end of the restraining ministry of the Holy Spirit at the Rapture of the Church.

The Apostle Paul wants us to make sure we understand what must happen for the Antichrist to emerge; Verse 2:8 reinforces that the Antichrist will not come to power until the evil-restraining ministry of the Holy Spirit ends. The Antichrist will establish a totalitarian government that will enslave the world. He will start out representing himself as a friend to Israel but will seek to destroy them and all who will not swear allegiance to him. God will tolerate un-throttled evil for only a short period to serve His purpose in pouring out His wrath. Ultimately God will defeat the Antichrist when Jesus returns to establish His Millennial Kingdom.

In verses 2:9-10, we learn that the Antichrist coming to power will be accompanied by great signs and wonders to deceive people into following him. God will allow deceptive miracles to dupe all who do not have the spiritual discernment that only comes from a relationship with Christ (see 1 Corinthians 2:14). Jesus warned about the coming deception of the Tribulation in Matthew 24:24. Already we can see the birth pangs of increasing deception that is leading astray all who are not well grounded in Christ.

6.2 Why God Allows Evil

Atheists often point to evil as justification for rejecting God saying, "how could a good God allow evil?" But those who question the purpose of evil don't understand the concept of sin. A just and holy God demands that there be consequences for usurping His authority. In a fallen world, evil happens as a consequence of sin.

People are made in the image of God (Genesis 1:26-27). One important aspect of that is God has given us the same freedom of choice He has. However, we have exercised our freedom to put ourselves before God despite the consequences of such selfishness. God loved us so much that He wanted us to experience the depth of relationship with Him that is only possible if we are free to accept or reject a relationship with Him. As Jesus said, *"I have come that they may have life, and that they may have it more abundantly"* John 10:10). If there is to be true free will, God has to allow evil for a time.

Despite there having to be evil so that we may have a true free will, God uses evil to help us. For example, He raised up the Babylonians to help Israel see their need to return to Him. He used the evil of Jesus dying on a cross to pay the penalty for our sins. He uses evil in our lives to bring about a greater good, *"we know that all things work together for good to those who love God, to those who are the called according to His purpose"* (Romans 8:28).

6.3 How God, the Holy Spirit Restrains Evil

God orchestrates events to bring about His plans (Isaiah 46:9-10). But God limits the reach of evil, as *"the LORD said to Satan, 'Behold, all that he has is in your power; only do not lay a hand on his person'"* (Job 1:12). While all of earth's rulers are under the influence of Satan, God influences their hearts so that His will be done. For example, this happened with the Persian King Xerxes in Esther 6 and the Roman Caesar Augustus prior to Jesus being born in Luke 2:1. *"The king's heart is in the hand of the LORD, like the rivers of water; he turns it wherever He wishes"* (Proverbs 21:1)

God also works through His children because the Holy Spirit indwells all who trust in Jesus for salvation (1 John 4:15). The Holy Spirit convicts God's children to expose evil; we are commanded to, *"have no fellowship with the unfruitful works of darkness, but rather expose them"* (Ephesians 5:11). Indeed, there will be loss of reward if we fail to speak up when we see evil (Ezekiel 33:9). Jesus said His followers are salt and light in Matthew 5:13-14; so we are called to act as a pre-servative helping others know Jesus and shinning the light of truth illuminating evil. Exposing evil does reduce it's impact, *"for everyone practicing evil hates the light and does not come to the light, lest his deeds should be exposed"* (John 3:20).

The U.S. has been known as a Christian nation because we have been the most preeminent Christian nation on earth. We were founded by Christians, made laws based on biblical values, and had the highest percentage of Christians among our citizens. We have promoted liberty and crushed tyrants who enslaved their people. We acted as God's agent to squelch the plans of the Nazis and their allies, the Soviets, and those who sought to enslave Africans. We have encouraged and helped Israel. Indeed, the U.S. has been a force for good in the world. President Ronald Reagan characterized America is a "shining city upon a hill" where people wanted to be and other nations wanted to be like.

But the U.S. is beginning to be less of a shining city on a hill fore-shadowing removal of the evil-restraining ministry of the Holy Spirit. The U.S. is known as much for our export of entertainment filth as we are for restraining evil in the world. We have legalized the murder of the unborn and now about 4,000 babies are killed in the womb every day. We have encouraged those who have sought to end the Bible's concept of marriage and have celebrated immoral lifestyles. We have institutionalized our national debt which is now on an exponential growth trend. We are abandoning our allies like Israel and embracing their enemies such as the Muslim Brotherhood. There is also a growing propensity to appease evil regimes and yield our sovereignty to the world community of nations. We are beginning to see our constitutional rule of law being replaced with rule of man and along with it, our freedoms of religion and speech are under assault. Truth and justice are being replaced with political correctness and so-cial justice which is simply a ruler's view of fairness. Our mainstream media no longer serves as a force which exposes evil, instead it is more of a propaganda agency seeking to manipulate people.

6.4 How We Know Evil is Being Restrained

The new normal seems to be the world living on the brink of disaster. Economic turmoil in various places threatens the stability of the world. The U.S. debt will eventually cause the dollar to no longer be the world's reserve currency so it too threatens world stability. Wars and rumors of wars rage in the Middle East. We seem to stay on the edge of war there due to Iran who believes it is their God-given mission to rid the world of Israel. The Muslim Brotherhood and Islamic State both share Iran's vision of a world without Israel and have taken over in multiple locations with designs on even more places.

Food shortages are emerging due to bad weather and bad governmental policies such as promoting corn ethanol instead of drilling for oil. Human caused global warming is being cited as the justification for bad energy policy. But this is really a contrived explanation to justify control of the energy which is necessary for freedom. The ultimate goal here is to increase centralized governmental control over the population. The trend toward totalitarianism will continue because the Bible says the world economy during the Tribulation will be under the Antichrist's total control (Revelation 13:16-17).

6.5 Antichrist in the News

The following topics often come up in the news revealing the growing spirit of Antichrist:

6.6 Growing Spirit of Antichrist

Evil men and impostors will grow worse and worse,
deceiving and being deceived (2 Timothy 3:13)

Satan is the father of lies (John 8:44) and thus the motivator of all deceptions (2 Corinthians 11:14). Those embracing evil and engaging in deception that serves the purposes of Satan will grow as we get closer to the return of the Lord. Jesus said the time-period leading up to His return would be *"as the days of Noah"* (Matthew 24:37) when evil abounded (Genesis 6:5).

The Holy Spirit is currently restraining evil but this ministry will cease with the end of the Church Age (2 Thessalonians 2:7). We are already seeing God's restraint on evil being removed. As we get closer to the return of Christ, this will become even more apparent as birth pangs herald the closeness of the Tribulation.

6.7 Change

He shall… intend to change times and law (Daniel 7:25)

As we get closer to the return of Christ, we can expect governments to deal with their troubles by making radical changes to our laws because the ruling elite conclude that the old ways must not work. These changes will cause chaos to reign as the stabilizing rule of law is replaced with the unpredictable rule of man.

6.8 Historical Revisionism

He shall... intend to change times and law (Daniel 7:25)

Along with changing law is changing times. As we get closer to the return of Jesus, more and more history will be rewritten to reflect badly on the old ways such as following the rule of law and embracing a biblical worldview. We are already seeing serious historical revisionism concerning the founding of the United States and in holocaust denial among Islamists. The popularity of Darwinian evolution is just another example of historical revisionism on a grand scale. Humanists in this postmodern age believe all history is suspect having been written to suit the perspectives of those who have prevailed in the conflicts with others. So since humanists are now gaining more power in our society with God removing His restraint of evil, they are taking advantage of their opportunity to re-write history to their liking.

6.9 Rule of Law Yielding to Rule of Man

The rulers take counsel together, against the LORD and against His Anointed, saying, "Let us break Their bonds in pieces and cast away Their cords from us." (Psalm 2:2)

As we get closer to the return of the Lord, we should expect the rule of law to be used less and less. All law is derived from God's Law which the Antichrist will seek to change. Psalm 2 goes on to relate the consequences of such opposition to God, they will be dashed to pieces.

6.10 Growing Lawlessness

Because lawlessness will abound, the love of many will grow cold (Matthew 24:12)

As we get closer to the return of the Lord, we should expect more lawlessness. Jesus told us that this growth of lawlessness would be a sign of His soon return. Such departing from God's Law will be accompanied by selfishness abounding and love growing cold. It is interesting to note that lawlessness will be personified in the Antichrist who is called *"the lawless one"* in 2 Thessalonians 2:8.

6.11 Growing Evil

"He who now restrains lawlessness is already at work"
(2 Thessalonians 2:7)
The Holy Spirit is restraining evil in this Age. But the day is coming when His ministry will cease. Evil will be allowed to have its day during the Tribulation accompanied by all of its consequences. As we get closer to the Tribulation, there will be less restraint of evil as birth pangs increase. These birth pangs serve to help the spiritually discerning know we are in the season of the Lord's return.

6.12 Growing Anarchy

God is not the author of confusion but of peace (1 Corinthians 14:33)
Ever wonder why the liberal mind abhors law and order? It is at its core rebellion against the Law Giver, God. So when the leftist media encourages people to riot in response to some perceived injustice or to rebel against the police who work to maintain the peace, recognize that they are simply exposing their hatred for God. Anarchists are always inspired by the devil with an insidious agenda behind them. In this stage of history, the local police are being ostracized to justify replacing them with a national, and ultimately a global police force. As all leftists will agree, you have to break a few eggs to make an omelet.

6.13 Growing Injustice

Even as they did not like to retain God in their knowledge,
God gave them over to a debased mind, to do those things
which are not fitting (Romans 1:28)
As we get closer to the return of the Lord, we should expect more injustice. In an age when we are seeing calls for social justice, true justice has to be sacrificed. God's law is just; man's rule is unjust due to sin. Sacrificing justice in order to satisfy man's idea of what is fair to one group means it has to be unfair to another. We can expect more irrational judgments as leaders get more ungodly.

6.14 Growing Rhetorical Deception

A mouth speaking pompous words (Daniel 7:8)

As we get closer to the return of the Lord, we should expect the character of the Antichrist to be more reflected in political leaders. The Antichrist will be charismatic and depend on oratory; he will be perceived as an eloquent, scholarly speaker. Thus political leaders most embraced by the public in the end times will likewise be those who speak with pompous words.

6.15 Growing Blasphemies

He shall exalt and magnify himself above every god,
shall speak blasphemies against the God of gods (Daniel 11:36)

As we get closer to the return of the Lord, we should expect more antichrist-speak from government leaders. Their huge pride will drive them to speak very highly of themselves and blatantly slander God as the Bible reveals Him. Politicians often give lip-service to the Bible by quoting Scripture but they usually have to take it out of context in order to justify their antichrist ideology. It is interesting to note that Satan used this same strategy when he tried to tempt Jesus in the wilderness (Matthew 4:6).

6.16 Growing Propaganda

The devil... does not stand in the truth, because there is no truth in him...
for he is a liar and the father of [lies] (John 8:44)

As we get closer to the return of the Lord, we should expect more deception from government leaders. In an age where there is growing support for the end justifying the means, it is more and more accepted that the government lying to the people is not such a big deal. Spin-doctors are praised as being shrewd manipulators of the public. So government leaders will get increasingly more deceptive and devoid of integrity. They will apply techniques like "The Big Lie" which Adolf Hitler described in his book, "Mein Kampf." Hitler found that if you boldly tell a big lie often enough, the public will come to believe the lie rather than consider that their beloved government would so blatantly mislead them. Every generation thinks they are smarter than the last and not subject to being manipulated by propaganda. The problem is that despite people thinking they are better than those who came before them, history still does repeat itself.

6.17 Fleeting Transparency

The beast which I saw was like a leopard, his feet were like the feet of a bear, and his mouth like the mouth of a lion (Revelation 13:2)

As we get closer to the return of the Lord, we should expect more camouflage to hide what government is really doing. The Antichrist will be ruthless, like an animal crushing all opposition to him. And part of his tactics will be to take people by surprise due to camouflage like a leopard. Increasingly we are seeing leaders saying things that sound good but doing the exact opposite of what they promised. Along with that, we are seeing more Orwellian language that masks the true intentions of government officials.

6.18 Growing Trickery

He shall come in peaceably, and seize the kingdom by intrigue (Daniel 11:21)

As we get closer to the return of the Lord, we should expect government leaders to use more deceptive tricks to obtain and retain power. The Antichrist will come to power *"by intrigue"* which according to the Blue Letter Bible Lexicon means by flattery, slipperiness, fine promises, and smoothness. The Antichrist will use deception and diplomatic trickery to catapult him to power. Dictators operate without public accountability because wickedness can not stand the light of scrutiny. Having a democracy is not an inoculation against despotism; Adolf Hitler was elected and the "Arab Spring" democratic movement only resulted in rule-of-man Islamists coming into power.

6.19 Growing Persecution

He shall speak pompous words against the Most High,
shall persecute the saints of the Most High (Daniel 7:25)

Jesus said His followers would be persecuted (John 15:20). He also indicated that persecution would be among the birth pangs that would herald the Tribulation (Matthew 24:9). Persecuting Christians is a symptom of the spirit of Antichrist and it will climax during the second half of the Tribulation.

6.20 Growing Invincibility

They worshiped the beast, saying, "Who is like the beast?
Who is able to make war with him?" (Revelation 13:4)

As we get closer to the return of the Lord, we should expect the agenda of anti-God government leaders to be harder and harder to stop. They will control people by fear and be so destructive that people will have no choice but yield to them. Satan is called Abaddon in Hebrew and Apollyon in Greek which means Destroyer (Revelation 9:11). Satan possesses the Antichrist and inspires all who have the spirit of Antichrist (Revelation 13:2).

6.21 Increasing Terrorism

Beat your plowshares into swords and your pruning hooks into spears;
let the weak say, "I am strong" (Joel 3:10)

This passage is talking about events leading up to the battle of Armageddon which is referred to in Joel as *"the Valley of Jehoshaphat."* (Joel 3:12). The context makes it clear that those who say *"I am strong"* are those who are gathering to do battle against God. They are finding their strength in themselves and not in God. This should be contrasted with the Christian attitude expressed by the Apostle Paul when he was coming to terms with his *"thorn in the flesh"* and he concluded, *"for when I am weak, then I am strong"* (2 Corinthians 12:10). The weak who say they are strong by turning plowshares into swords and pruning hooks into spears are terrorists. They take peaceful tools of productivity and turn them into weapons. This is what the weak, deceived people did on 9/11 turning a passenger airliner into a guided missile. And they think they have power because of this. Expect this type of terrorism to increase as we get closer to the Tribulation.

6.22 Growing Socialism

He shall do what his fathers have not done, nor his forefathers: he shall
disperse among them the plunder, spoil, and riches (Daniel 11:24)

Socialism will be the economic system of the Antichrist. Totalitarian control is his objective and is required to make socialism work. The problem is that socialism never works as well as it sounds in theory; what could be more fair than everyone having the same income? In reality socialism robs the successful and distributes their wealth to the lazy thus stifling innovation and fostering mediocrity. Spreading the wealth around sounds good but it oppresses people, enslaving them to the state. As we get closer to the time of the Antichrist, we can expect the trend toward socialism to accelerate.

6.23 Growing Economic Destruction

He shall destroy many in their prosperity (Daniel 8:25)

Oddly enough, wealthy people are all on-board with the trend toward socialism. They have theirs and they know money buys them favor that they can leverage for even more money. The ruling class always does well when they have more control over the public. But this means an end to the middle class which gives the poor hope to improve their condition. With socialism there is no hope for the masses, just shared misery. But the wealthy elite who think they will have an advantage with socialism will find that what they have been hoping in will let them down. These wealthy elite will be regarded as "useful idiots" to advance the agenda of the Antichrist only to find that they themselves are caught up in the destruction that follows.

6.24 Compromise

A little leaven leavens the whole lump (Galatians 5:9)

Leftists increasingly complain that conservatives will not work with them, accusing them of being unreasonable because they will not compromise with them. They say that is how our system is supposed to work. But it has become apparent that a process of compromise is how we got to where we're at in the U.S. today. As long as there is compromise with the left, we are always advancing the leftist agenda. If our compromises are always increasing the debt, the debt will continue to grow. Rather than compromise with evil, those on the side of Righteousness need to stand firm and not compromise with the ways of the world. *"Resist the devil and he will flee from you"* (James 4:7).

7 GLOBALISM

Globalism is a major trend prophesied in Scripture. When Jesus returns, there will be a global government, religion and economy. There is evidence of progress toward this every day in the news. As national sovereignty is yielded to the world community of nations, individual freedoms are being lost. The struggle over immigration policy is also discussed in this chapter as an important facet of globalism.

One of the more obvious trends in the end times is the growth of globalism. As "thinking globally" becomes more pervasive, it will only be natural for people to embrace a global government. It is true in this world that power corrupts and absolute power corrupts absolutely; so we can expect global power to corrupt totally. The coming global government will be totalitarian. Indeed, Satan hates the freedom we have in Christ and seeks to enslave everyone to him.

Among the trends toward globalism is the decline of the United States as a superpower. Just as the superpower stand off with the Soviet Union during the Cold War had to be resolved, so too does the last superpower have to be diminished in order to make way for a global government. The U.S. had once been the bright shining light of freedom on earth and this is increasingly under assault as a birth pang of the Tribulation.

The following are topics that often come up in the news revealing the trend toward globalism:

7.1 United Nations

All the world marveled and followed the beast. (Revelation 13:3)

73

The stage is being set for a worldwide government in the United Nations. As this forum of nations grows in influence, it will provide the infrastructure for a global government. The U.N. was established after World War II as an organization to help us avoid more war. But the U.N. has grown in influence finding itself getting involved in all manner of issues between nations. Eventually there will be some crisis that will make it even clearer that the world needs a global government.

7.2 Global Government Trend

The kings of the earth set themselves, and the rulers take counsel together, against the LORD and against His Anointed (Psalm 2:2)

The Bible says there will be a global government in place prior to the return of Jesus. There is a relentless trend toward a worldwide government. Besides the UN growing in influence, we have the model of the European Union (EU) demonstrating that it is possible to have "unity in diversity." And we have the U.S. no longer acting unilaterally in foreign affairs, the U.S. must only act as part of the community of nations.

There is also a relentless trend toward bigger government as the solution to all of societies' ills. Eventually some crisis either real or fabricated will cause the public to be convinced that our huge national government is not large enough spurring the call for a global government as the ultimate Big Government solution. We already have a worldwide economy where if an individual nation's finances get sick, the affliction quickly spreads to the whole global organism.

7.3 Antichrist Rules Over a Global Government

Authority was given him over every tribe, tongue, and nation.
(Revelation 13:7)

The coming global government of the Tribulation will be headed by the Antichrist. The world is rapidly headed toward a one-world government as prophesied in the Bible. Europe is leading the trend for diverse nations to set aside their national sovereignty for the greater good (Revelation 17:13). We have global trade that needs to be regulated and worldwide problems such as terrorism and global warming that are beyond any single nation to resolve by itself. Since the trend toward globalization is obvious to all, tension has emerged between those who would like to retain national sovereignty and those who think we should yield to the community of nations in order to facilitate the coming glories of the global village. God says a global government will come, resistance is futile.

7.4 Global Religion Trend

Then I saw another beast... he exercises all the authority of
the first beast in his presence, and causes the earth and those
who dwell in it to worship the first beast. (Revelation 13:11-12)

During the Tribulation, there will be a global religion in place headed by the Antichrist *("beast")* and helped by the False Prophet *("another beast")*. The False Prophet will probably represent himself as Jesus Christ to cause apostate Christians to get on-board with the new world religion. Jesus warned that there would be those falsely representing themselves as the Christ during the Tribulation (Matthew 24:5). In order for the whole earth to worship the Antichrist, all religions will have to consolidate. We already see that in universalism which promotes the idea that all religions worship the same God just by different names and in different ways. But Jesus made it clear that universalism is a false doctrine when He said; *"I am the way, the truth, and the life. No one comes to the Father except through Me"* (John 14:6).

7.5 Global Economy Trend

He causes all, both small and great, rich and poor, free and slave,
to receive a mark on their right hand or on their foreheads, and that
no one may buy or sell except one who has the mark or the name
of the beast, or the number of his name. (Revelation 13:16-17)

There will be a centrally controlled global economy during the Tribulation. Some crisis will cause people to clamor for big government administration that will be exploited by the Antichrist. Daily there are new developments moving us closer to a more centralized global economy. For example, there is the phenomenon of multinational corporations in our day. Notice that in the U.S. we are no longer preventing companies from becoming "too big to fail." Once upon a time we broke-up potential monopolies. Instead, we are accom-modating Big Business and letting them grow larger than the Gross National Product of many nations. Consolidation at the mega-corporation level is never a good thing; it centralizes control over markets and reduces competition making for fewer consumer choices. Growing government regulations to protect huge corporations from competitors is an attack on free-market capitalism and is the result of cronyism in the government-industrial complex.

7.6 Global Conspiracies

For we do not wrestle against flesh and blood, but against principalities, against powers, against the rulers of the darkness of this age, against spiritual hosts of wickedness in the heavenly places. (Ephesians 6:12)

The trend toward a global government is so pervasive that some have blamed conspiracies. Secretive groups such as the Bilderbergers, Trilateral Commission, and Council on Foreign Relations are accused of being cabals of government elites conspiring to consolidate their power globally. What is more likely is that the globalism trend is a result of spiritual warfare with government leaders being tempted by demons to take actions that set the stage for a global government. Indeed, Jesus referred to Satan as the ruler of this world (John 14:30 and 2 Corinthians 4:4). It is interesting that when Satan tempted Jesus in the wilderness, he offered up all the kingdoms of the world if Jesus would worship him (Matthew 4:8-9). Jesus did not dispute that Satan had control of all the nations in the world. There is a global conspiracy but it is not a human one so much as it is a spiritual one.

7.7 Failure of Human Government

For all have sinned and fall short of the glory of God (Romans 3:23)

People have made their government into an idol, as if their government can deliver them from whatever afflicts them. But human governments in this age are made up of people with a sin nature and so they will eventually fail. The more people trust in their government, the more they are destined for disappointment. Satan is encouraging the failure of governments to move us toward more centralized control. As governments fail, they need to be bailed out by yet a higher echelon of government. We should work to reduce the failures of government but at the same time acknowledge that what this world sorely needs is for Jesus Christ to head our government. This is not a desire for self-fulfilling prophecy with a theocracy, it is hope for the supernatural intervention of God in the Millennial Kingdom.

7.8 Fleeting National Sovereignty

These are of one mind, and they will give their power
and authority to the beast (Revelation 17:13)

A major trend leading to global government is that more and more national sovereignty is being given up to the collective community of nations. This is particularly apparent in the U.S. where people are increasingly more willing to yield their freedoms to satisfy demands of a growing centralized government. As we get closer to the Tribulation, the incidence of birth pang crises will increase providing more opportunities for governments to take more freedom from the public. The ruling elites have learned not to let a good crisis go to waste. As every level of government seeks help from higher governmental authorities, eventually there will be a clamor for a global government as more nations need help.

7.9 Fleeting Freedom of Speech

You shall know the truth, and the truth shall make you free (John 8:32)

As we get closer to the Tribulation, we can expect the loss of rights we enjoy like the freedom of speech. The U.S. media used to speak truth to power but this check on government abuse is no longer working as reporters have become more committed to leftist causes. God's enemies hide the truth so people have no choice but to go along with their evil plans. Silencing voices of opposition is what totalitarian dictators do and is a powerful oppressive tactic in the spirit of the Antichrist.

7.10 Fleeting Freedom of Religion

He was given a mouth speaking great things and blasphemies
(Revelation 13:5)

As we get closer to the Tribulation, we can expect there to be less freedom of religion. America is following Europe in the secularization of our society. Evolution, a materialistic worldview of origins not requiring God prevails in the culture so pervasively it is more of a religion than a theory. The media increasingly represents Christians as ignorant undesirables holding society back. The spirit of Antichrist demands that all people conform to their politically correct beliefs and believing the Bible has no place in where they want to take society.

7.11 Enhanced Interrogation

If anyone does not provide for his own, and especially for those of his household, he has denied the faith and is worse than an unbeliever (1 Timothy 5:8)

People were all up in arms about the U.S. government using water boarding and other psychological techniques to coerce information from captured terrorists in the wake of 9/11. These enhanced interrogation techniques were labeled torture and decried as a terrible thing for a civilized nation to be engaged in. But these techniques were not torture because they did not cause any permanent damage to the terrorists and the information that was obtained saved lives. Thus, enhanced interrogation is a legitimate way to gain intelligence in order to protect our citizens. Those who oppose enhanced interrogation are collaborating with the forces trying to reduce the power of the United States. The idea that the U.S. must have less security in order for the world to have more security reveals an irrational globalist mindset in the spirit of Antichrist.

7.12 Immigration Reform

He has made from one blood every nation of men to dwell on all the face of the earth, and has determined their preappointed times and the boundaries of their dwellings (Acts 17:26)

God intends for the nations to control their borders. Immigration should be orderly and serve the interests of the nations involved. Ignoring the established borders is the result of a globalist worldview that seeks to undo what God has established. Open borders immigration is just one more facet of the spirit of Antichrist. The coming global government will not have any effective borders between nations. Those who seek to open the national borders are longing for the global government that sets the stage for the Antichrist.

7.13 Immigration and Security

Unless the LORD watches over the city, the watchmen stand guard in vain (Psalm 127:1, NIV)

Calls to control immigration as a hedge against terrorism are irrational and reveal a humanist worldview. The real source of a nation's security is the providence of God. We need to do our due diligence to maintain security but, at the same time recognize that ultimately God is in control. Let's not lose sight of the real source of our nation's security. When we are attacked, God allows this to happen for a reason; it should shake us up enough to draw closer to Him and seek His deliverance.

7.14 The Christian and Immigration

When an alien lives with you in your land, do not mistreat him. The alien living with you must be treated as one of your native-born. Love him as yourself, for you were aliens in Egypt. (Leviticus 19:33-34, NIV)

As God brought people to Israel so that they could learn about Him and be saved, the U.S. is one place in the world where this can happen today. We don't have to go to all the world to teach the gospel if representatives from all the world come here. Indeed, people come to the U.S. because of the freedoms we enjoy that facilitate prosperity. With the declining birth rates in the United States, we need some way to keep the population (and economy) growing. So the Christian should take full advantage of helping immigrants to know Christ as the source of our freedoms while this is still possible. The day is coming when our freedoms will evaporate with the U.S. becoming just another state in the global government.

8 THE NATIONS

The Nations are becoming aligned as they will be during the Tribulation as an important sign of Jesus returning. This chapter discusses Nebuchadnezzar's dream which reveals the nations that would rule over the world from Jerusalem's perspective. The end times wars of Ezekiel 38 and Psalm 83 are also addressed. The Abrahamic Covenant is related to the Middle East peace process and multiple examples are given of the United States suffering consequences from forcing Israel to surrender land for peace.

Closely related to globalism is what is going on among the nations of the world. As God said, *"Look among the nations and watch-- be utterly astounded! For I will work a work in your days which you would not believe, though it were told you"* (Habakkuk 1:5). We know we are getting closer to the return of the Lord when we see the nations setting the stage for the Tribulation.

To better understand how we got to where we are today in world politics, it is helpful to look at what has happened in history. The Bible has a lot to say about world politics in history from Israel's perspective. And, given the importance of Israel in God's eye (Zechariah 2:7-8), looking at history from Israel's point of view is the most important perspective to have.

8.1 Nebuchadnezzar's Dream

You, O king, were watching; and behold, a great image! This great image, whose splendor was excellent, stood before you; and its form was awesome (Daniel 2:31)

One of the most amazing episodes giving insight to world history is described in Scripture where the prophet Daniel interprets a dream of King Nebuchadnezzar of Babylon (Daniel 2). The prophecy of nations that would rule over Jerusalem described in this dream was so exact that some skeptics have insisted the book of Daniel had to be written much later than what biblical scholars say.

King Nebuchadnezzar dreamed of a statue with a head of gold, a silver chest and arms, a bronze belly and thighs, legs of iron, and feet of iron mixed with clay. A *"stone not cut out by human hands"* struck the statue at its feet and became a great mountain that *"filled the whole earth"* (Daniel 2:32-35).

God revealed to Daniel the interpretation of the dream that the head of gold represented Babylon and King Nebuchadnezzar in particular. The silver chest and arms represented a kingdom that would *"arise"* after Babylon which would be succeeded by another kingdom represented by the bronze body parts and so on. Daniel explained that the *"stone not cut out by human hands"* represented a Kingdom established by God that would never end. From other passages of Scripture, we know this is the Millennial reign of Christ on earth that will extend into the Eternal State.

From history, we know that the silver chest and arms represented the Medes and Persians. Two arms represent two peoples working together to defeat and replace the Babylonians. History also tells us the Greeks, represented by the bronze belly and thighs in the dream succeeded the Medes and Persians again through conquest. The Romans represented by the legs of iron defeated the Greeks. We should also note that the Romans had two major branches, the Western leg based in Rome and the Eastern leg based in Constantinople. They started out as two legs of the same government, just as in the dream.

The Western leg of the Roman Empire fragmented into city-states of Europe then became nations that colonized a large part of the world. The United States started as a colony of Great Britain and assimilated colonies of Spain and France having a form of government that borrows heavily from the Romans. Even the architecture of the official buildings in Washington D.C. reveals a Roman influence. So the iron in the feet of the statue in Nebuchadnezzar's dream was a continuation of the Roman Empire. The more the former Roman nation-states work together as part of NATO and now the

European Union, the more people are coming to recognize the rise of a Revived Roman Empire.

The Eastern leg of the Roman Empire morphed into the Byzantine Empire which was conquered by the Ottoman Empire that ruled over much of the Middle East until WW I. Effectively, the Ottoman Empire was an Islamic successor to the Eastern Roman or Byzantine Empire in ruling over Jerusalem. So the clay in the feet of the statue of Nebuchadnezzar's dream represents the Ottoman Empire. While the Ottoman Empire does not exist today, there are multiple Muslim jihadist groups actively working to reinstate an Islamic caliphate just as there was during the Ottoman Empire. Since these diverse Muslim groups agree on the vision of an Islamic caliphate, we effectively already have a Revived Ottoman Empire.

The history of the Roman and Ottoman Empires satisfies Daniel's prophecy of the iron and clay where they did not *"adhere to one another, just as iron does not mix with clay"* (Daniel 2:43). Rule over Jerusalem has oscillated between the remnants of the old Ottoman and Roman Empire until Israel regained authority over Jerusalem in 1967. While Israel annexed Jerusalem, they allowed the Islamists to continue ruling over Temple Mount, the spiritual heart of Jerusalem. So Jerusalem continues to be trampled on by the remnants of the old Ottoman Empire; thus we are still in the *"times of the Gentiles"* (Luke 21:24).

The last human government ruling over Jerusalem when the Messiah returns is represented by the kingdom of iron mixed with clay. Even the ten toes in the dream have symbolic relevance here since Revelation 17:12-13 tells us there will be ten kings ruling the world who yield their authority to the Antichrist. No-doubt these ten kings will emerge from remnants of the old Roman and Ottoman Empires.

The Prophet Daniel's interpretation of Nebuchadnezzar's dream has been validated by history, so we should expect the rest of it to happen just as foretold. As we see the stage being set for its fulfillment, we know we are close to Jesus returning for His own.

8.2 Pursuing Peace

For when they say, "Peace and safety!" then sudden destruction comes upon them, as labor pains upon a pregnant woman. And they shall not escape. (1 Thessalonians 5:3)

The nations seek after peace. They long for the day when *"they shall beat their swords into plowshares, and their spears into pruning hooks"* (Isaiah 2:4). The nations think they can achieve peace through human means; if all parties can just sit down together, be reasonable and talk about their differences. But humanism does not recognize the root problem of sin that plagues mankind (Jeremiah 17:9). All human efforts to bring peace between the nations will continue to fail. Indeed, such efforts will in fact make matters worse. By pursuing peace apart from God, Israel will effectively be making a pact with Satan which will result in condemnation and more death (Isaiah 28:15-18). The peace that the nations pursue will be a peace that would *"destroy many"* (Daniel 8:25). There will be no peace until the return of Jesus, the *"Prince of Peace"* (Isaiah 9:6).

8.3 End Times Wars

You will hear of wars and rumors of wars (Matthew 24:6)

There will be a lot of warfare during the Tribulation and there will also be birth pangs of war leading up to this terrible time. There are a couple of wars in the time-frame of the return of Jesus described in Scripture that may even happen prior to the Tribulation. Certainly as we see the alliances of the nations involved in these wars forming up, we can expect to be getting very close to the Tribulation.

8.4 Magog War, Ezekiel 38-39

Russia

There will be a major war in the Middle East when Russia attacks Israel probably as a pretense to control Middle East oil supplies (Ezekiel 38-39). *"The word of the LORD came to me: "Son of man, set your face against Gog, of the land of Magog, the chief prince of Meshech and Tubal"* (Ezekiel 38:1-2, NIV). Magog is an ancient reference to the peoples north of the Black Sea, or Russia. If there is any doubt that this is referring to Russia, Ezekiel 38:6 and 38:15 clears this up saying they come from the *"far north."* Any world map will reveal that the only major city to the *"far north"* of Jerusalem is Moscow which is directly north.

The leader of Russia (Magog) is called Gog and is described as a *"chief prince"* in Ezekiel 38:1-2. It is amazing how the *"chief prince"* title describes Vladimir Putin who as Prime Minister was the leader of

Russia even when Dmitry Medvedev was the president, a mere puppet of Putin.

The Lord compels Russia to attack Israel: *"I will turn you around, put hooks in your jaws and bring you out"* (Ezekiel 38:4, NIV). Ostensibly, Russia invades the Middle East to help their allies with their "Israeli problem" but their real agenda is to gain control of Middle East oil so that they may dominate the world. Russia has come to understand how market economies work from first-hand experience. The key to dominating the world is to control the oil that market economies need to flourish.

Today, we see the stage being set for this incredible prophecy about the time leading up to the return of Israel's Messiah (see also Ezekiel 37). The time-frame is given in Ezekiel 38:8, after Israel has been gathered from many nations and is back into their land. This can not be referring to the return from Babylon or Assyria as amillennial preterits would say because of the reference to *"many nations."*

Per Ezekiel 38:2 and 38:5, the following modern countries are allied with Russia against Israel:

- **Armenia** called Meshech
- **Georgia** called Tubal
- **Iran** called Persia
- **Sudan** called Cush
- **Libya** called Put
- **Turkey** called Gomer and Beth Togarmah

We certainly see these alliances forming today.

The timeframe for the Magog War is after Israel is back in the land having been re-gathered from dispersion, *"brought out of the nations"* (Ezekiel 38:8). They also *"dwell safely"* which probably means they live in a false peace that the Antichrist will confirm for them (see Daniel 9:27). Israel is described as a *"land of unwalled villages"* (Ezekiel 38:11) so their false peace must be enough to get them to dismantle their security walls. Such conditions indicate that the Magog War will likely happen during the Tribulation though that is not necessarily the case.

Ezekiel 38:13 lists some nations that question the Russian alliance attacking Israel:

- **Saudi Arabia, Yemen** called Sheba
- **Kuwait** called Dedan

- **Spain, Europe** called Tarshish
- **USA, European Colonies** called Tarshish villages

It is also possible that the USA is represented in Ezekiel 39:6 where the Magog War escalates to a nuclear exchange: *"I will send fire on Magog and on those who live in safety in the coastlands, and they will know that I am the LORD"* (Ezekiel 39:6, NIV). Most of the population of the U.S. is on the Atlantic, Pacific, Gulf of Mexico and Great Lake coasts. People wonder why a superpower such as the U.S. doesn't have a more prominent role in end time events; this may be why. The fire on Magog and the coastlands may be supernatural but the usual pattern of God is to work through natural means so those who've rejected Him may continue in unbelief. The fact that this was foretold in ancient times makes it supernatural.

8.5 Psalm 83 War

There is likely to be a war in the Middle East that precedes the Ezekiel 38 Magog War which has to occur when Israel is living at peace. This can hardly be described today with their having to use security fences to keep the suicide bombers away. It is also interesting to note that the nations coming against Israel in Ezekiel 38 are not the ones immediately surrounding and threatening them today.

Psalm 83 describes an alliance between the enemies of Israel which is referred to as God's people under His protection (Psalm 83:3). The motivation of the enemies of Israel is the very same as we see in Hamas, Hezbollah, Islamic State and the Muslim Brotherhood today: *"Come, and let us cut them off from being a nation, that the name of Israel may be remembered no more"* (Psalm 83:4).

The nations and people-groups allied against Israel for this war are given in Psalm 83:6-8:

- **Jordan** called Edom, Ammon, and Lot
- **Arabs** called Ishmaelites.
- **Egypt** called Moab and Hagrites. See also *"the burden against Egypt"* in Isaiah 19.
- **Lebanon** called Gebal and Tyre
- **Anti-Semites** called Amalek
- **Gaza** called Philistia
- **Syria & Iraq** called Assyria

8.6 Syria: Burden Against Damascus

Damascus will no longer be a city but will become a heap of ruins
(Isaiah 17:1, NIV).

The capital of Syria is Damascus which boasts that it is the oldest, continuously inhabited city in the world. But the Bible says this will come to an end some day. It is likely that a nuclear weapon will be used to destroy Damascus. Turmoil in Syria will eventually blow up and engulf Israel. Syria is aligned with Iran and harbors Hezbollah, Iran's proxy. Hezbollah has attacked Israel before and they will again. There is also the Muslim Brotherhood-inspired Islamic State stirring up the region in their effort to establish an Islamic Caliphate. Syria's chemical weapons have supposedly been destroyed but who knows if all of them really were? What will Israel's response be if missiles with chemical warheads are launched from Syria into Tel Aviv?

The Psalm 83 War may be a good time for the Rapture of the Church. The Rapture must occur prior to the Antichrist stepping forward to guarantee peace for Israel. What better time for the Rapture to occur than during some world-wide crisis like a nuclear war? The use of a nuclear weapon will be a major distraction for the world. In light of such a tragedy, who would miss the disappearance of a few million Christians?

8.7 The Palestinians

Your enemies make a tumult; and those who hate You
have lifted up their head (Psalm 83:2)

The term "Palestinian" is effectively another reference to Arabs, the descendants of Ishmael. There were no people of Palestine in history. The term Palestine was chosen by the British to describe the land around the Jordan River and west to the Mediterranean Sea. The term "Palestine" is derived from the term "Philistine" which referred to non-Israelites of the Promised Land during the days of Samson, Saul and David.

8.8 China

The great river Euphrates... was dried up to prepare the way
for the kings from the East. (Revelation 16:12, NIV)

During the Tribulation, a two hundred million man army will invade the Middle East probably to secure the oil supply they need (Revelation 9:14). This 200M-man army will end up killing a third of the earth's population per Revelation 9:15. This occurs just before the final battle of Armageddon per Revelation 16:12-16.

8.9 United States

The instant I speak concerning a nation and concerning a kingdom, to pluck up, to pull down, and to destroy it, if that nation against whom I have spoken turns from its evil, I will relent of the disaster that I thought to bring upon it (Jeremiah 18:7-8)

While the United States is not specifically mentioned in Scripture, there are principles that have been given to Israel which apply to all nations. The United States has a special burden to follow the decrees of God because of the blessings we have received. As we have as a nation moved further from God, our blessings are beginning to be removed. You'd think this would shake us up and cause us to repent but we continue on the broad humanist way. The U.S. was shaken by the attack on our country 9/11/2001 but the turning to God lasted about a month. Unfortunately, we can expect all the wrath God poured out on Judah to be visited upon this country.

8.10 Covenant Consequences

Now the LORD had said to Abram: "Get out of your country, from your family and from your father's house, to a land that I will show you. I will make you a great nation; I will bless you and make your name great; and you shall be a blessing. I will bless those who bless you, and I will curse him who curses you; and in you all the families of the earth shall be blessed." (Genesis 12:1-3)

One of the most important promises God has made in Scripture is the Abrahamic Covenant. This promise was reinforced and amplified in Genesis 13, 15, 17 and 22. All-told, the Abrahamic Covenant had fourteen unconditional provisions that effectively were prophecies:

1. Abraham would become a great nation
2. Promised land: Canaan
3. Abraham would be greatly blessed
4. Abraham's name would be great
5. Abraham would be a blessing to others
6. Those who bless Israel would be blessed
7. Those who curse Israel would be cursed
8. Through Abraham all humanity would be blessed

9. Abraham would receive a son of promise by Sarah
10. Abraham's descendants would undergo bondage in Egypt
11. Other nations would come from Abraham
12. Abram's name would change to Abraham (father of many nations)
13. Sarai's name would change to Sarah
14. Circumcision would become the sign of the covenant

All of the prophecies in the Abrahamic Covenant have been fulfilled in history with most of them still actively being fulfilled. For example, the descendants of Abraham continue to be a blessing to people. All of Scripture was written by the descendants of Abraham. The greatest blessing to mankind ever, Jesus Christ was a descendant of Abraham. There are people yet to be born who will be blessed by the descendants of Abraham. So the prophecies that are ongoing also represent promises that tell us what we can expect from God. The most relevant promise or prophecy for the discussion that follows is that those who curse Israel will be cursed by God.

Besides the passages in Genesis directly addressing the Abrahamic Covenant, there are many other places in Scripture that these promises are applied. One of the applications of this promise is a prophecy of Israel in the end times that also gives us a warning about trying to keep God from fulfilling His promises to Israel:

For behold, in those days and at that time, when I bring back the captives of Judah and Jerusalem, I will also gather all nations, and bring them down to the Valley of Jehoshaphat; and I will enter into judgment with them there on account of My people, My heritage Israel, whom they have scattered among the nations; they have also divided up My land. (Joel 3:1-2)

What is trading land for peace in Israel if not *"dividing up"* the land God has given Israel? There has been an amazing correlation of national catastrophes in the U.S. with our forcing Israel to give land away. Naturalists will dismiss these as being mere coincidence but those with a biblical worldview know better. The following are some examples of direct consequences to the U.S. as a result of coercing Israel in the pursuit of peace:

8.11 The Perfect Storm

President George HW Bush first outlined a plan of trading land for peace in a speech at the Madrid Conference October 30, 1991. That same day, an "enormous extra tropical low" combined with a tropical cyclone, became a hurricane that was called the Perfect Storm with wind at 120 MPH and waves ten stories high. The storm traveled 1,000 miles from east to west which is very rare in that part of the Atlantic Ocean. They even made a movie about the storm featuring the loss of the Andrea Gail. The storm severely damaged President Bush's house at Walkers Point in Maine just hours after his speech. President Bush had to cancel a speaking engagement to inspect the damage done to his home. The irony was that with Bush touching God's land, God touched Bush's land.

8.12 Hurricane Andrew

Pressure from U.S. bilateral talks resulted in a new Israeli government which capitulated on August 24, 1992. That same day Hurricane Andrew smashed into Florida making it the most destructive natural disaster to hit the U.S. up to that time. At land-fall, Andrew was a Category 5, 177 MPH storm with a 17-foot storm surge. It left 200,000 people homeless, killed 65, and damages exceeded $38B. There were also 152,000 people without power and it destroyed twenty-five percent of the trees in everglades. Ninety percent of the homes in Dade county had roof damage with 117,000 homes destroyed or with major damage. Homestead Air Force base was closed as a full active duty base due to damages.

8.13 Trade Center Bombing

President Clinton's Secretary of State Warren Christopher held a joint news conference with Prime Minister Yitzhak Rabin to announce their commitment to land for peace on February 24, 1993. They would be meeting for two more days in private talks to work out the details. On February 26, 1993 while Christopher was in the air going back to the U.S., a bomb hid in a yellow Ryder van exploded in the World Trade Center. This bomb opened up a 98-foot wide hole through four sub levels of concrete and was intended to bring down the North Tower in such a way to also bring down the South Tower. Six people were killed, a thousand were injured, smoke filled up the building to the 93rd floor, and power was knocked out to

Lower Manhattan cutting off most of the city's radio and TV stations. Now we can see this as a warning foreshadowing the destruction of the World Trade Center buildings September 11, 2001.

8.14 Midwest Flooding

President Clinton, Prime Minister Yitzhak Rabin, and Palestinian leader Yasser Arafat met in Norway to announce what became known as the Oslo Accords on September 13, 1993. The talks leading up to the agreement went from April to August that year. Following the agreement, Israel pulled their military units from the Gaza Strip and West Bank (Judea) despite Palestinian attacks against Israel intensifying. While these talks were going on, the U.S. experienced record flooding from May to September across North and South Dakota, Nebraska, Kansas, Minnesota, Iowa, Missouri, Wisconsin and Illinois. Up to thirty-six inches of rainfall occurred in some areas which were 200-350% of normal. Fifty deaths occurred with damages on the order of fifteen billion dollars. Hundreds of levees failed on the Mississippi and Missouri rivers. This was the most significant flood to ever occur in the U.S. with 10,000 homes being destroyed and tens of thousands more having to be evacuated. Seventy-five towns were completely under flood waters and fifteen million acres of farm land was inundated, some of which would not be useable for years. Barge traffic was halted for two months, ten commercial airports had to close, interstate highways were closed, and rail traffic in the Midwest was halted.

8.15 Clinton Impeachment

In January, 1998 President Clinton met with Prime Minister Netanyahu and Yasser Arafat to "jump start" the peace process. In this meeting Clinton pressured Netanyahu to surrender 13% of the West Bank and on January 20, Clinton was to have a working lunch with Netanyahu to work out the details. When Israel refused to surrender any land, Clinton terminated the meeting and Netanyahu left unfed and diplomatically insulted. The next day, independent counsel Ken Starr who had been commissioned to look into the Whitewater scandal and Vince Foster suicide was authorized to expand his investigation to look into pressure on a Whitehouse intern to lie to lawyers for Paula Jones about an affair with the president. This exposed the president's affair with Monica Lewinsky. The irony was that 24 hours after the President threatened Netanyahu with his job; his own political career was threatened. Clinton tried to head off the impeachment vote by launching a military strike against Iraq on December 19, 1998 but became the first elected U.S. president and second president to be impeached by the U.S. House of Representatives.

8.16 9/11 Attack

In 2001, Crown Prince Abdullah of Saudi Arabia expressed dismay to President G. W. Bush that he was not confronting Israel about their "overly" aggressive response to terrorism and threaten to cut off communications with the White House. President Bush responded by sending the Crown Prince a letter August 29, 2001 agreeing that he would support an independent homeland for the Palestinian people. Bush agreed to come out publicly about this the week of September 10, 2001. Bush, V.P. Cheny, Secretaries Rice, Powell, and Ambassador Bandar met on September 7, 2001 to work out the details of the Bush announcement. They met through the week-end and completed the plan to establish a Palestinian state in Israel by 2005. Secretary Powell was to present the plan at a U.N. General Assembly meeting two weeks later. All this was put on hold because on September 11, 2001 more Americans died by jihadists than at Pearl Harbor in 1941 or the D-Day invasion (2,977, 2,350 and 1,465 respectively).

8.17 Hurricane Katrina

The U.S. pressured Prime Minister Ariel Sharon to use 14,000 soldiers and police to evict Israeli settlers in twenty-one compounds from Gaza on August 15, 2005. This resulted in 2,700 homes being bulldozed and 9,000 Israelis were forced out. By August 22nd, the last settlers had been removed and Bush congratulated Sharon in a speech. On August 23rd, a tropical depression formed near the Bahamas which became Hurricane Katrina. The storm crossed Florida as a Category 1 hurricane but strengthened in the Gulf of Mexico to Category 5 with winds at 175 MPH. Katrina then went into New Orleans forcing a million Americans from their homes. There were over 225,000 homes in three states destroyed with over $150 billion in losses, the most expensive natural disaster in American history.

8.18 2008 Recession

President G. W. Bush proposed a peace conference in Annapolis, Maryland where Secretary Rice hinted that Israel was prepared to give up all the West Bank including parts of Jerusalem in return for peace on November 27, 2007. Palestinian President Abbas said that only giving up the West Bank in its entirety would be acceptable. Prime Minister Olmert indicated that he would be willing to give up some of the West Bank but not all of it. An agreement between the parties was negotiated in bi-weekly meetings and they were prepared to announce it on September 16, 2008 at the U.N. General Assembly. But on September 15th, troubled real estate assets became apparent causing the Dow to fall 777 points; the largest single-day decline since the great depression. This then plunged the world into recession and the U.S. rushed approval of a $700 billion bail out package for banks "too big to fail." This and subsequent new loans would cost the U.S. Treasury, Fed, and FDIC over five trillion dollars. The irony here is that while the world intended to celebrate the capitulation of Israel, we instead suffered a devastating collapse of our equity markets.

8.19 "New Normal" Continuing Recession

President Obama has maintained the pressure on Israel to give up more land for peace. To his credit, Prime Minister Netanyahu has resisted these attempts showing that he is wise to this losing game. But President Obama's actions did serve to encourage "Arab Spring" revolts which replaced dictators with radical Islamists. This president has been officially supportive of the Muslim Brotherhood and is committed to only weak sanctions against Iran signaling to Israel that they will be on their own militarily against existential threats. So we are continuing in our financial Tribulation: high unemployment, wages declining, inflation looming, foreclosures and bankruptcies up, retirement savings loss of value, and debt on an exponential growth curve. We have been told this is the new normal; perhaps it is with the growing anti-Semitism in the world.

8.20 Hurricane Sandy

Some may ask why the 2012 Hurricane Sandy is not included here but it did not have a direct connection with the U.S. pressuring Israel. Not all our disasters are due to the U.S. abusing Israel. If that was the case, the correlation would be a bit too obvious and God is way too subtle for that. However, it is interesting to note that Sandy was predicted to make landfall exactly 21 years from the anniversary of the Perfect Storm. Twenty-one is a factor of three and seven; in the Bible the number three relates to God and seven is related to "completion." Hurricane Sandy hit us a week before the presidential election but there was no significant difference between the candidates "official" position toward Israel. Maybe all Hurricane Sandy did at the end of a billion dollar Presidential campaign was to remind us who is really in charge.

8.21 Supernatural Intervention

Some naturalists will balk at this evidence for God intervening supernaturally in our affairs insisting on some sort of scientific statistical analysis. But that will not help them see what is going on here. These were just antidotal examples of events that are beyond coincidence. People insisting on applying the scientific method here are free not to believe the supernatural was involved and it is their choice to continue in unbelief. Being free to continue in unbelief is why a statistical analysis will never give 100% certainty that selected acts of God are directly correlated to Israel abuse. God is subtle so that people are free to continue in their unbelief if that is their desire; note that Jesus often spoke in parables for just that reason, see Matthew 13:10-13. Thus God does speak to us in probabilities, 100% certainty is not required for the spiritually discerning. We can however be 100% certain that the prophecies in Scripture will be fulfilled exactly as they were given to us.

So are these examples just interesting coincidences or something else? God is at work fulfilling His promises. He is warning us to realize before it is too late that He is still intervening in our world and embrace His plan for us. In the New Covenant, God promised an eternal relationship with Him for all who accept the provision He made for our sins to be forgiven (Matthew 26:27-28). What a blessing! Who wouldn't want to appropriate this wonderful promise of God? The only people who would consider rejecting the Lord are those with a humanist worldview who are so full of themselves they don't have room for God in their lives.

9 ISLAM

Islam has emerged in prominence as jihadists work to realize their vision of the world being united under their religion. The Bible tells us there will be a global religion of the Antichrist and we can see the stage being set for this in Islam. The demonic origin of Islam is discussed in this chapter along with prophecies that are being fulfilled by Muslims daily in the news.

The amazing growth in influence of Islam is a critical sign of the times. Those professing Islam comprise about 22% of the global population and is growing while those professing Christianity is about 32% and dropping. Islam wasn't really on the radar screen in the United States until 9/11/2001. Since then, it has caused the U.S. to spend its blood and treasure to keep terror groups from being a bigger problem than they are. The political correctness associated with appeasing Islamists is stunning. No one wants to give Islamists an excuse to "radicalize," as if that is what caused 9/11 to happen.

9.1 Moderate Islam

The conventional wisdom is that Islam is a religion of peace; that moderate Muslims who consider jihad to be only a spiritual struggle is the norm. While most Muslims are cultural and not religious, those who do truly embrace Islam and begin following what the Quran actually says are compelled to kill infidels for Allah. The Quran commands violence: *"Fight and slay the pagans (infidels) wherever ye find them, and seize them, beleaguer them, and lie in wait for them in every stratagem of war"* (Sura 9:5). Islam also teaches that the only way a follower can know he is going to paradise is to die in the process of killing infidels. That is why Islam is the perfect religion to motivate suicide murdering terrorists. The Quran commands its followers to be terrorists: *"Let not the unbelievers think they will ever get away... strike terror into the enemy of God and your enemy... rouse the faithful to arms!"* (Sura 8:59).

Islam is really a very bloody religion. The word "Islam" means "submission." Muhammad received the inspiration to write the Quran while under the "submission" of an angel. If the Sharia Law of the Quran is resisted, a bloody penalty is called for: *"Their punishment is execution, or crucifixion, or the cutting off of hands and feet from the opposite sides, or exile from the land"* (Sura 5:33).

9.2 The Coming Al Mahdi

The worldwide growth of Islam has caused the nations to work together more in order to combat terrorism. This is just one more factor contributing to the globalism of the nations. But Islam has an even greater role in end times events. It is interesting to consider what Islamists expect for the culmination of history. Muslims expect their messiah, al Mahdi (meaning "one of the moon"), will return in the midst of world turmoil to unite the world under Islam. This al Mahdi will be assisted by the return of the prophet Jesus who will convince Christians that the Bible was corrupted and that they should follow al Mahdi. There are striking parallels between al Mahdi and the Beast of Revelation as well as the Islamic prophet Jesus and the False Prophet of Revelation. So it is likely that the worldwide religion of the Antichrist is some amalgamation of Islam and apostate Christianity.

Another indication that Islam will be a major factor in the end times world religion of the Antichrist is the judgment that God declares on so many Islamic nations in Scripture. Over and over again, God proclaims *"the burden against"* nations that are now Islamic: Egypt (Isaiah 19), Babylon (Isaiah 13), Edom (Isaiah 21:11), Arabia (Isaiah 21:13) and Syria (Isaiah 17).

9.3 Islamic Symbols

There are a growing number of religious leaders who proclaim that the Muslim god Allah is the same as the God of the Bible. Anyone who truly knows the God of the Bible knows this can not be the case. Islamists do not recognize Jesus as God, the Son; they think He was just a prophet like Muhammad. Instead they worship a god of human creation derived from Bel, the moon god Babylonians worshipped which had a crescent moon as an emblem. In pre-Islamic Arabia, Allah was recognized as a moon god before Muhammad declared he was the only god. Since Islamists worship a demonically inspired, human-created concept of god, they are idolaters in Gods eyes per Exodus 20:3.

Another symbol of Islam is a star depicted with the crescent moon. Islam began as an eastern religion and the east is where the morning begins, hence the "morning star." It is interesting to note that Satan is also called Lucifer which means "morning star" or "son of the morning star." This reveals a lot about Islam: *"How you are fallen from heaven, O Lucifer, son of the morning! How you are cut down to the ground, you who weakened the nations!"* (Isaiah 14:12).

Along with the symbols of Islam, Muhammad instituted green as the color of Islam because he described paradise as being filled with green and the people there would wear green garments of fine silk. Thus the dominate color on most of the flags of Islamic countries is green. It is interesting to note that the fourth horse of the Apocalypse (Revelation 6:2-8) is described in most English Bible translations as being pale, but the original Greek word is *"chloros"* which is translated *"green"* wherever else it is used. The colors of the four horses of the Apocalypse are significant and there is no such thing as a green horse. The first white horse carries a leader appearing to be a "good" guy (the Antichrist); the second red horse represents a lot of blood shed due to war; the third black horse represents a scarcity of basic necessities; and the fourth green horse is a key to the religion that inspires all the killing.

9.4 Demonic Origins

Islam is an end times doctrine of demons which is designed to lead people away from the God of the Bible (1 Timothy 4:1). It has been used by Satan to deceive and control people on a large scale: *"For Satan himself transforms himself into an angel of light"* (2 Corinthians 11:14). It is thus interesting to note that the Quran refers to Allah, the god of Islam, as *"the great deceiver"* (Surah 3:54).

The way of salvation for the Muslim is in stark contrast to biblical Christianity. As with all human-created religions, Islam is very works-based. Islam requires their followers to earn salvation by observing the "Five Pillars of the Faith" though dying while waging jihad is the only certain way to heaven. With Christianity, it is trust in the work of Christ on the cross that makes it possible for His followers to go to heaven. *"In Him we have redemption through His blood, the forgiveness of sins, according to the riches of His grace"* (Ephesians 1:7).

The following are some likely news topics related to Islam that the Bible addresses:

9.5 Islamic Deception

The devil... is a liar and the father of it (John 8:44)

Islam has a concept called "taqiyya" which encourages Muslims to be deceptive to further their religious cause. It is part of the Islamic culture to lie about their religion to outsiders. It boggles the mind how people taught to hide the truth can believe their religion is from God and reveals its demonic origins.

9.6 Religion of Peace

You will know them by their fruits (Matthew 7:16)

Given that Islamists are taught to use deception as a tactic to further their cause, you can not rely on what they say to the public about their religion, you have to watch what they do. It is politically correct to claim that Islam is a religion of peace. Since virtually all terrorism is inspired by Islam, you have to wonder on what planet the politically correct pundits are talking about when they call Islam a religion of peace. When Muslims talk of peace, they are referring to their version of peace they expect to exist when the world is united under Islam. They know that will only happen through violent jihad and threatening or killing non-Muslims to coerce them to convert or die.

While the Quran is contradictory about peace, Islamists invoke the "Law of Abrogation" which teaches that later verses advocating violence supercede the earlier passages speaking of peaceful coexistence. Either the talking heads trumpeting the peacefulness of Islam are trying to appease Muslims out of fear or they identify with their cause. It doesn't really matter which it is, the result is the same.

9.7 Islamic Terrorism

The time is coming that whoever kills you will think that he offers God service (John 16:2)

Are there any other religions that command their followers to kill unbelievers? Islam is the only religion that institutionalizes killing as a way to force converts. Thus Islam is the most likely candidate to be the religion of the Antichrist.

9.8 Terror Tactics

Proclaim this among the nations: "Prepare for war! ...beat your plowshares into swords and your pruning hooks into spears; let the weak say, 'I am strong.'" (Joel 3:9-10)

Islamic terrorist tactics reveal the religion of the Antichrist because the context of this passage in Joel is the battle of Armageddon, see Joel 3:12. Terrorists take peaceful tools of productivity (plowshares and pruning hooks) and turn them into weapons (swords and spears). Thus a passenger airliner becomes a guided missile enabling the weak to claim power over the strong. And dying in the service of Allah is powerful motivation to inspire suicide murderers.

9.9 Terror Weapons

Inventors of evil things (Romans 1:30)

Islamic terrorists have become very good at bomb making. Satan has enticed them to channel their creativity into inventive ways to bring destruction. The fact that Islamist don't know how to build up but sure know how to tear down speaks volumes of their religion. The Muslim ingenuity is clearly in the spirit of Antichrist who gets his inspiration from Apollyon, another name for Satan meaning Destroyer (Revelation 9:11). Yet the multiculturalists embrace Islam as having something positive to offer society.

9.10 Swords Used in Executions

Behold, a pale (green) horse... power was given to them over a fourth of the earth, to kill with sword (Revelation 6:8)

It has been a long tradition within Islam to kill with the sword, even in these modern times. Indeed, the Muslims' favorite way to kill infidels is to behead them with a sword. We also find that symbols of swords are on many Islamic flags.

9.11 Famine in Islamic Regions

Behold, a pale (green) horse... power was given to them over a fourth of the earth, to kill... with hunger (Revelation 6:8)

Have you ever considered why most famines occur where Islamists are active? It isn't a matter of there being enough food in the world to feed the hungry; it is a problem of distribution. And Islamists use this as a way to control people and to kill their political enemies.

9.12 Islamists Pursuing WMDs
Behold, a pale (green) horse... power was given to them over a fourth of the earth, to kill... by the beasts of the earth (Revelation 6:8)
Islamic jihadists are always pursuing more ways to make a bigger impact with their terrorism. So that is why they covet getting their hands on weapons of mass destruction. The poor man's WMD is a biological weapon using bacteria or viruses that are very small *"beasts of the earth."*

9.13 Islamists Killing Christians
I saw under the altar the souls of those who had been slain for the word of God and for the testimony which they held. (Revelation 6:9)
It is significant that this verse is found immediately following the revelation of the fourth, green horse of the Apocalypse. Tribulation Martyrs slain for their testimony of God are most likely victims of the onslaught of the green Islamic machine.

9.14 Islamists Beheading Infidels
Then I saw the souls of those who had been beheaded for their witness to Jesus and for the word of God (Revelation 20:4)
Beheading will be the most common way martyrs are killed during the Tribulation. It is interesting to note that the favorite method of execution by Muslims just happens to be how most of the Tribulation martyrs will be killed. This alone is enough to tell us the growing impact of Islam is a key end times trend.

9.15 Islamists Killing Islamists
He shall be a wild man; his hand shall be against every man, and every man's hand against him (Genesis 16:12)
Islam started among the Arabs who where descendents of Ishmael, the illegitimate son of Abraham. The prophecy in Genesis 16:12 is very accurate. When Islamists are not out killing "infidels" they are killing each other. Most of the world's Muslims are Sunni as observed in Saudi Arabia where Islam began. But there is also Shia Islam which looks to Iran for leadership. While these two major sects of Islam

have their differences, they agree on their mandate to wage jihad on Israel and Western Civilization.

9.16 Islamic Antichrist

After the sixty-two weeks Messiah shall be cut off, but not for Himself; and the people of the prince who is to come shall destroy the city and the sanctuary (Daniel 9:26)

In context, the *"prince who is to come"* refers to the Antichrist and he is of the people who destroyed Jerusalem and the temple in 70 A.D. History tells us that the Roman army did this; Josephus said it was the Fretensis (10th) legion that destroyed the temple. While the Roman 10th legion had Roman leadership, it was made up of soldiers from what is now Syria and Turkey. So this should lead us to expect the Antichrist to come from this region which may mean he will be Muslim. However since the Roman connection is also seen here, it could be that he will be from a Western nation. Wherever he is from, he will certainly have plenty of appeal to the Islamic world.

9.17 Revived Ottoman Empire, Islamic Caliphate

There are also seven kings. Five have fallen, one is, and the other has not yet come. And when he comes, he must continue a short time. And the beast that was, and is not, is himself also the eighth, and is of the seven, and is going to perdition (Revelation 17:10-11)

This passage gives another clue that the Antichrist (Beast) could come from an Islamic culture. When this was written, the Egyptians, Assyrians, Babylonians, Persians, and Greeks had fallen. Rome was the one that "is" and they morphed into the Byzantine Empire which was the Eastern leg of the Roman Empire. The one that would come best describes the Ottoman Empire as the seventh head ruling over Jerusalem. The eighth kingdom ruling over Jerusalem will be a revival of the seventh, the old Turkish Ottoman Empire.

9.18 Clay Kingdom

Whereas you saw the feet and toes, partly of potter's clay and partly of iron, the kingdom shall be divided; yet the strength of the iron shall be in it, just as you saw the iron mixed with ceramic clay (Daniel 2:41)

The Ottoman Empire took over the Byzantine leg of the Roman Empire by military conquest. This was the same for each of the kingdoms that have ruled over Jerusalem. There were also many times in the history of the Ottoman Empire that they were allied with the remnants of the Roman Empire. Throughout their history, the land ruled by the Ottomans and Rome jockeyed back and fourth from the time the Ottomans came on the scene up until Israel regained authority over Jerusalem in 1967. Israel let the Islamists hold onto the Temple Mount so technically the heart of Jerusalem is still being *"trampled by Gentiles"* (Luke 21:24).

9.19 Terrible but Weak Government

As the toes of the feet were partly of iron and partly of clay, so the kingdom shall be partly strong and partly fragile. (Daniel 2:42)

As the materials in the statue in Nebuchadnezzar's dream got progressively less valuable, each succeeding government gets weaker. There is inherent weakness in democracies as opposed to monarchies. Indeed, the two independent iron and clay governments have not been effective in ruling over Jerusalem. This has contributed to Israel and the Palestinians haggling over who controls what in Jerusalem.

9.20 Roman and Islamic Democracy

As you saw iron mixed with ceramic clay, they will mingle with the seed of men... (Daniel 2:43)

The best explanation of this is that both the iron and clay kingdoms will be democratic. Unlike the former kingdoms, the rulers of the iron mixed with clay kingdoms will be subject to the people they rule. This is certainly the case with Turkey and the European Union today.

9.21 Islam versus Western Civilization

As you saw iron mixed with ceramic clay... they will not adhere to one another, just as iron does not mix with clay (Daniel 2:43)

The rule of the Temple Mount in Jerusalem will vacillate between the Revived Roman and Ottoman empires *"until the times of the Gentiles are fulfilled"* (Luke 21:24). These cultures not being able to mix will cause there to be conflict between the forces of Islam and Western Civilization until Christ returns to end all wars.

While Islamists have enclaves in Western nations and visa versa, there is virtually no assimilation either way. And this mixing is causing strife, particularly in the European nations that have a lot of Muslim immigrants. These countries have now realized that they have brought jihad to their homeland by opening their borders to Muslim immigrants.

9.22 Temple Mount Mosque

Jerusalem will be trampled by Gentiles until the times
of the Gentiles are fulfilled (Luke 21:24)

Until Israel took Jerusalem in 1967, it was ruled over by all the Daniel 2 empires. However, we are still in the times of the Gentiles because the Temple Mount is still under Gentile (Islamic) control. Nonetheless, the Bible says that Israel must have a temple in Jerusalem during the Tribulation in order for the Antichrist to commit the *"abomination of desolation"* (Matthew 24:15; Daniel 9:27, 11:31, 12:11).

9.23 Islamic Antichrist Type

They shall defile the sanctuary fortress; then they shall take away the daily
sacrifices, and place there the abomination of desolation (Daniel 11:31)

Preterits are amillennialists who believe most prophecies of Christ's second coming have been fulfilled in history. They like pointing to the time that Antiochus Epiphanies slaughtered a pig to Zeus on the temple altar in 167 BC as fulfillment of the *"abomination of desolation"* prophecy. But this can not be the fulfillment because in context, it has to occur in conjunction with the return of the Messiah to establish His Kingdom on earth. Jesus said the *"abomination of desolation"* would happen during the Tribulation (Matthew 24:15). Instead, Antiochus Epiphanies is a type of the Antichrist which serves to give us more evidence of the Islamic background of the Antichrist. It is interesting to note that Antiochus Epiphanies came from the Seleucid division of the Grecian Empire that was stationed in today's Turkey, Syria and Iran.

9.24 Sharia Law

He shall speak pompous words against the Most High, shall persecute
the saints of the Most High, and shall intend to change times and law
(Daniel 7:25)

A major characteristic of Islamic nations is the implementation of Sharia Law which foreshadows what the Antichrist will do. The Antichrist will change laws that have been derived from a biblical worldview, and this is what Sharia Law does. So it is likely that the Antichrist will implement some derivative of Sharia Law. The spirit of Antichrist is seen in Sharia Law with its death penalty for blasphemy which is defined as mocking Islam and its prophet Mohammad. Islamic nations also change their calendar from one based on the birth of Christ to the Islamic calendar which began when Muhammad emigrated from Mecca to Medina. We can expect the Antichrist to throw out anything inspired by Christ.

9.25 Crusades Against Islam (Daniel 7:25)

Apologists for Islam love to point out that Christianity had a violent past with the Crusades and Inquisition. But any research of the true history beyond the superficial would reveal that the Crusades were a response to Islamic jihad spreading into Europe. Historical revisionists like to paint the Crusades as expansionist imperialism but their purpose were actually intended to discourage Islamists from invading Europe and open Middle East Christian holy places again to pilgrimage. Likewise, a serious unbiased investigation into the Inquisition would reveal that the Catholic Church had virtually nothing to do with it. It was the secular authorities who burned the heretics seeing heresy as treason because royal authority was questioned. These same secular authorities criticized the church for not taking a more active role in the Inquisition.

Of course humanists don't really care much about history. They are quick to dismiss history saying, "the winners get to write the history" which is just a rationalization to ignore history. Since today's postmodern humanists believe that history is subject to interpretation, they set out to change the record of history by advancing a narrative that makes Christianity out to be a villain. Such historical revisionism is in the spirit of Antichrist which is growing in our day.

It is pretty clear to those who watch current events without a humanist bias that virtually all the terrorism going on in the world is due to Islam despite the media trying to put lipstick on the pig. Humanists will say this is evidence that Christianity is just more evolved than Islam, that we just need to be patient with them until they have their reformation. But this only reveals the continuing ignorance of history that characterize humanists. The Protestant Reformation wasn't about repenting of a violent past, it was about returning to biblical authority. Christianity never had a history of pursuing conversions through violence as Islam practices.

As radical humanists are allowed to have more power in this

world, there will be more historical revisionism to stir up the public to turn further from God and His children. Since we are in the season of Christ's return, we can expect the spirit of Antichrist to build culminating in the person of the Antichrist coming to power. Thank God the Church will not be on earth when the Antichrist reigns. Now is not a good time to be on the fence about Jesus as Savior.

9.26 Human Rights
There is neither Jew nor Greek, there is neither slave nor free, there is neither male nor female; for you are all one in Christ Jesus (Galatians 3:28)

It is amazing that the world embraces Islam under the umbrella of cultural diversity with the way it treats women. Cultural diversity only gives people an excuse to turn away from the God of the Bible because they want to be their own authority. Islam institutionalizes abuse of women treating them like property. The Islamic oppression of women is evidence that this religion was inspired by demons. More evidence is the fact that Islamic countries don't tolerate any other religions; they have to be that way because if people were truly free to chose they'd chose anything but Islam, especially the women.

9.27 Political Left Aligning with Islam
For God has put it into their hearts to fulfill His purpose, to be of one mind, and to give their kingdom to the beast (Revelation 17:17)

The political left will not admit that they are aligning themselves with Islam but actions speak louder than words. You would think the way Islam treats Jews, Christians, women and gays, the left would be a mortal enemy of Islam but that is not the case. There are more shared ideals between the political left and Islam than there are disagreements so the leftists are very accommodating toward Islamists. Both are totalitarian in wanting to control all aspects of human existence. Both are anti-capitalist and regard individuals as only existing to serve the collective. Both see the U.S. freedom culture with individual liberties as an obstacle and want to fundamentally change or replace Western Civilization.

9.28 Muslim Conversions
I will pour out My Spirit on all flesh; your sons and your daughters shall prophesy, your old men shall dream dreams, your young men shall see visions (Joel 2:28)

While missionaries are forbidden in many Islamic nations, this has not kept God from revealing Himself to people in those nations. Revelation 5:9 tells us that God will save people from all nations. He prefers to bless His followers by involving them in the process but when Satan's followers keep that from happening, God's will is still done; *"I will do all My pleasure"* (Isaiah 46:10). There are many testimonies on You Tube and other places of people from Islamic nations who came to Christ as a result of a direct revelation from Him. Jesus Himself appeared to them in a dream or a vision and they responded to Him even under penalty of death in those countries. God is preparing to reap a great harvest from every nation!

10 THE ECONOMY

The Economy is already global and will be the tool the Antichrist uses to control the world. The Bible has a lot to say about the economy of the Tribulation and we can see the stage being set for this daily in the news. The trends toward more centralized control, socialism, growing debt, inflation, and economic exploitation are all discussed in this chapter.

While the economy is a global trend, it stands out as its own separate category because there is so much going on in this area that reveals our closeness to the Tribulation. The following are topics that often come up in the news regarding trends in the economy:

10.1 Growing Socialism

He shall do what his fathers have not done, nor his forefathers: he shall disperse among them the plunder, spoil, and riches (Daniel 11:24)

As we get closer to the return of the Lord, we should expect governments to become more socialistic. The ultimate goal of socialism is totalitarian control because this is required to fully implement socialism. Since socialism never works, more and more control is necessary to inflict it on people. The Antichrist will help selected people prosper by "spreading the wealth around." He will use his total control to steal from some and give to certain favored groups. In socialism there can be no private property, everything is owned by the government for the sake of the "greater good" and subject to the whims of the ruling elite.

10.2 Biblical Socialism

Now all who believed were together, and had all things in common, and sold their possessions and goods, and divided them among all, as anyone had need (Acts 2:44-45)

Socialists love to cite the Bible to justify their ideology because the early Christians shared their possessions with the community. But serious Bible students know that one must be very careful building doctrine from the book of Acts. The reason is that Acts records a time that was very unique in the history of the church when the disciples were still performing miracles of the sort that Jesus did. These miracles were intended to authenticate God's spokesmen and reinforce what God was saying while the canon of New Testament Scripture was still being written. Things were very different in the Church in those days to the point where people died when they lied about their good deeds (Acts 5:1-11). The Apostle Paul said that the sign gifts of the disciples would cease when the New Testament canon of Scripture is complete (see 1 Corinthians 13:10 in context).

Another reason the communal economy of the First Century Jerusalem Church can not be used to justify socialism is that the giving was totally voluntary. With socialism, the "giving" is mandatory.

10.3 Socialism Opposes God

If anyone will not work, neither shall he eat (2 Thessalonians 3:10)

God's economy is based on merit and is far from socialism. It is ironic that socialists try to justify their policies using the Bible when it is obvious they hate God. Socialists see themselves in competition with God because they want the government to be the provider and savior of the people. And their ideology is rooted in sin: *"You shall not covet your neighbor's house… nor anything that is your neighbor's"* (Exodus 20:17). Socialists oppose the freedom and independent spirit that comes from having a relationship with God. God created each of us unique with diverse gifts that can best be applied when people are free to do what God has called them to. When the government mandates what a person can and can not do, innovation is crushed.

Karl Marx, the father of socialism, summed up his spread-the-wealth-around ideology with the statement, "from each according to his ability; to each according to his need." This is in stark contrast to what Jesus told us of God's view: *"to one he gave five talents, to another two, and to another one, to each according to his own ability"* (Matthew 25:15).

God allocates abilities according to His purposes and God-given abilities are revealed in productivity. Thus the free market is the best arbiter of who gets what resources, not some bureaucrat who seeks to act in the place of God.

10.4 More Centralized Control
No one may buy or sell except one who has the mark or the name of the beast, or the number of his name (Revelation 13:17)
The coming economy of the Antichrist during the Tribulation will mean total control of the economy worldwide. As we get closer to the Tribulation, we will see more consolidation of economic control, such as banks that are "too big to fail." The mark of the beast will force people to swear allegiance to Antichrist in order to participate in the economy. During the Tribulation, people must have the mark of the beast in order to buy groceries. Of course followers of Christ and honest seekers of Truth will know better than to take this mark because it will seal their eternal fate (Revelation 14:9-10). The best way to avoid the pressure to take the mark of the beast is to be a follower of Christ before the Church Age ends.

10.5 Another Government Program
You shall take no bribe, for a bribe blinds the discerning and perverts the words of the righteous (Exodus 23:8)
It seems as if the proliferation of government programs is accelerating in our day. If society has any perceived need, there is some centralized government program for it. Government programs mean government money and who can turn down free money? But it's not free, it puts the pressure on raising taxes and increases the debt which will cause the purchasing power of money to be reduced. Oh, and it has strings attached. The government does not provide funds without mandating how the funds are to be used. The government money is really about control. Often crony capitalism is involved where there is a pay-off to political friends, or social engineering where an approved group is being compensated for some perceived injustice, or it constitutes an out-right bribe for votes. There is increasing pressure for the government to control every aspect of our lives because the day will come when the Antichrist will have worldwide totalitarian control.

10.6 Tax the Rich

The rich shall not give more and the poor shall not give less than half a shekel, when you give an offering to the LORD (Exodus 30:15)

A fair tax is a flat tax where everyone pays the same tax rate. But in these days of growing socialism, there are increasing calls to increase the tax rate on the rich which is already progressive. This sounds fair because the wealthy are always somebody else. The problem is that there really are not enough rich people to cover all the funds needed for government programs so the taxes always trickle down to the working class. Since greater taxes have the impact of reducing a person's freedom, higher taxes are really about the government controlling people. And as the freedoms of wealthy people are restricted, they make fewer job-creating investments. Of course the ruling class thinks it is government programs that create jobs so we can expect that eventually everyone will be working for the government, the ultimate goal of socialism.

10.7 Increasing Greed

With eyes full of adultery, they never stop sinning; they seduce the unstable; they are experts in greed—an accursed brood! (2 Peter 2:14, NIV)

While free market capitalism is generally superior to socialism, some have corrupted it out of their greed. Liberal rationalizations lacking a moral compass have institutionalized greed as being good for the economy. All the economy needs is for consumers to ratchet up their consumption so people are encouraged to live beyond their means. Investors are taught to leverage "other people's money" by pursuing as much debt as they can convince others to give them. Our buy now, pay later economy is enslaving people and sapping their freedom (Proverbs 22:7).

10.8 Economic Bubbles Forming

You shall carry much seed out to the field and gather but little in, for the locust shall consume it. (Deuteronomy 28:38)

As God used pestilence to discipline Israel's agrarian economy, He allows recessions to occur in our economy to serve His purposes. The frantic focus on accumulating wealth by a few in one sector devours wealth for the many in other sectors creating financial bubbles that are doomed to burst. We have seen financial bubbles in technology, real estate, oil, credit, and food just to mention a few.

10.9 Economic Bubbles Bursting

He shall destroy many in their prosperity (Daniel 8:25)

As we get closer to the return of Jesus, there will be more events that wipe out wealth for a growing number of people. Ideologies associated with the spirit of Antichrist like socialism will accelerate this trend. Satan will take advantage of people trusting in worldly resources for their deliverance. As we get closer to the Lord's return, there will be an increasing number of occasions for people to put their trust in God instead of their bank accounts.

10.10 Growing Wealth Gap

Through his cunning he shall cause deceit to prosper under his rule
(Daniel 8:25)

The gap between rich and poor will become greater the closer we get to the return of Christ. The spirit of Antichrist which seeks to spread the wealth around only enables the wealthy to get wealthier and the poor to get poorer. God-hating leftist ideologies always make worse the very problem they are trying to fix. You would think the history of failures for socialism would cause people to run away from it but government elites think they can be smarter than all others that have tried it before them. Or they think that maybe a little socialism will help; the problem is that it never does and the only solution they can come up with is just a little more socialism. As has been rightly said, "the definition of insanity is doing the same thing over and over again expecting different results."

10.11 Inflation

A quart of wheat for a day's wages, and three quarts of barley for a day's wages, and do not damage the oil and the wine! (Revelation 6:6, NIV)

The economy during the Tribulation will get so bad that most people will be living paycheck to paycheck, working just to eat. There are many people in the world living like that now but this will apply to an increasing number of people as we get closer to the Tribulation. Food will be expensive because demand will outstrip the supply. Wars, pestilence, socialism, and centralized control will devastate food production and distribution.

10.12 Fleeting Supplies

Lift up your eyes to the heavens, look at the earth beneath;
the heavens will vanish like smoke, the earth will wear out
like a garment and its inhabitants die like flies. (Isaiah 51:5, NIV)

The earth is changing due to pollution, forests are disappearing, fish stocks are being depleted, and the oil age is coming to an end being accelerated by the fear of global warming. One sign that we are nearing the end of the age is that the earth's supply of resources can not keep up with demand from the increasing population. All but the well seasoned truth-deniers can see that we are headed toward some sort of culmination of history.

Whether the earth's oil supply is really drying up or whether political agendas are keeping oil from being produced, the effect is the same. The ruling class humanists impose their uninspired solutions on the public making matters worse.

It is no accident that most of the world's oil supplies are in the Middle East. Approximately 75% of the world's oil is in Islamic countries. Eight of the ten largest oil producing nations are Muslim. Muslim nations use 15% of the oil of citizens in the ten richest Western nations: Australia, Belgium, Canada, France, Germany, Italy, Netherlands, Spain, UK, and USA. This supply and demand imbalance is sure to exacerbate tensions in a region already prone to sectarian conflicts.

10.13 Growing idolatry

No one can serve two masters... you cannot serve God and mammon.
(Matthew 6:24)

Greed is often the motivation for accumulating more wealth than is needed. And in an age were the end justifies the means, greed leads to unfair practices that hurt others. Mammon represents the spiritual forces leveraging the lusts of the world to diminish God's glory. Thus the pursuit of wealth for any reason other than God's glory is idolatry. Scripture didn't say wealth is a problem, but rather the pursuit of it (2 Timothy 6:10). Satan heartily endorses anything that detracts from God.

10.14 Growing Debt

The rich rules over the poor, and the borrower is servant to the lender.
(Proverbs 22:7)

Satan loves to enslave people and nations. That is why there is so much more individual and national debt as we get closer to the Tribulation. As people get further from God, they depart from the principles He gave us to keep out of trouble, like living within our means. The ruling class in the U.S. pursues national debt with a passion that defies all logic. It is as if they don't think there will be any consequences. This betrays their humanist worldview which has no concept of sin. Debt always means enslavement.

10.15 Growing Humanism

The heart is deceitful above all things, and desperately wicked;
who can know it? (Jeremiah 17:9)

Virtually all liberal leftists are at their core humanists. This ideology thinks that man can make his own way in the world without God and has no concept of sin. Because humanists do not account for the natural depravity of mankind, it always catches them by surprise when their social programs do not work. A good example of this is the uninspired idea that everyone in America should own a home. The economic crash of 2008 was brought on by humanists making home mortgage credit approvals into a social program.

10.16 Growing Exploitation

You have heaped up treasure in the last days; indeed the wages of the
laborers who mowed your fields, which you kept back by fraud, cry out
(James 5:3-4)

As we get closer to the Tribulation, an increasing number of common wage earners will be taken advantage of. The lust for more wealth or the appearance of wealth (credit) has caused people to make immoral decisions to satisfy their own greed. The reason why wealthy men support socialism is not to "spread the wealth around," it is to control the wealth. Socialism has never been a movement of the people though "useful idiots" may be employed to give it that appearance; it is really pushed by the economic elite to have control over the public.

10.17 Growing Inflation

The wicked borrows and does not repay (Psalm 37:21)

Debt is borrowing from the future to have something today. The U.S. government uses statistical trickery excluding "volatile" commodities to lie about how much inflation there really is. All the while the cost of living steadily increases. Inflation is a hidden tax; as the government prints more money and goes further into debt, the purchasing power of the money is reduced. Inflation causes a person's life's savings to be worth less and less thus making more people dependant on the government; and this is just where we're wanted by the spiritual handlers pulling the strings of the ruling class.

10.18 The Final Economic Crash

The merchants who sold these things and gained their wealth from her
will stand far off, terrified at her torment. They will weep and mourn…
In one hour such great wealth has been brought to ruin!
(Revelation 18:16-17, NIV)

During the Tribulation, the world's economy will get so bad that it will suffer a non-recoverable catastrophic crash. The idol of mammon will come crashing down. All the stock market corrections, recessions, and depressions we have had were just birth pangs leading up to the big one that will devastate the world. Nothing can be done to prepare for this other than to know Jesus as your Savior.

10.19 God Controls the Economy

For every beast of the forest is Mine, and the cattle on a thousand hills.
(Psalm 50:10)

Ultimately, God is in control of the resources in this world (see also Revelation 4:11). God owns it all and He is in control of the economy allowing it to be in a state that serves His purpose. He has allowed supply and demand imbalances to develop to bring about the course of events foretold long ago.

10.20 Don't Fear the Coming Crash

The cries of the harvesters have reached the ears of the Lord Almighty
(James 5:4, NIV)

Those who trust in Jesus don't have to fear the coming economic crash. We know that the Lord will return to bring justice to the earth thus fixing the economy. When He rules on earth during the Millennial Kingdom there will be just compensation for honest work (Isaiah 65:22-23).

10.21 God Promised to Sustain Us

As long as the earth endures, seedtime and harvest, cold and heat,
summer and winter, day and night will never cease (Genesis 8:22, NIV)

God has promised that He will not interrupt His provision for us. As there have always been agricultural cycles, there will also be economic cycles. Our economy today is a global economy. God promised continued general (or world-wide) prosperity for the agrarian economy following the global flood. The principle here is good news that today's global economy will continue to grow despite set-backs foreshadowing the Tribulation. As there have been agricultural cycles since Bible times, we have always had economic cycles as well. The great economic crash of Revelation 18 will occur during the Tribulation and that will not happen as long as the Church is on the earth.

10.22 Business as Usual During the Church Age

As in the days before the flood, they were eating and drinking, marrying
and giving in marriage, until the day that Noah entered the ark
(Matthew 24:38)

Until the Tribulation, all economic perturbations will be minor enough that generally life will continue as normal for all practical purposes. All of the stock market crashes, recessions and depressions we go through are just birth pangs and are manageable to those who apply God's principles. That will not be the case during the Tribulation. So it is much better to allow Christ into your life during the Church Age rather than risk waiting until the Tribulation.

If the economy is getting worse, Christians should rejoice recognizing that this helps set the stage for the Tribulation. Since the Rapture of the Church precedes the Tribulation, this means Jesus is getting ready to Rapture us! If the economy is getting better, Christians should rejoice realizing that the Tribulation may be further away than we thought; so there may be more time to help others know Jesus! *"Rejoice in the Lord always. Again I will say, rejoice!"* (Philippians 4:4).

11 GLOBAL WARMING

Global Warming is man's explanation for increasing instances of record-breaking weather events. Those who believe that it is the activities of mankind causing these developments pursue draconian reduction of carbon dioxide emissions with religious fervor. But the Bible tells us what is really going on revealing that the fear of global warming is a byproduct of people not knowing Jesus Christ as their Savior.

It does appear as though extreme weather is on the increase. Many think it's because of global warming. Those who study the Polar Regions have been raising alarms that the ice fields are shrinking. But global warming is controversial because the average temperature of the planet really has not changed much.

Those who insist that global warming is occurring say mankind is the cause due to the greenhouse effect from increasing carbon dioxide. Others oppose this because of the economic ramifications citing the average global temperature data and recognizing that varying solar radiation is a bigger factor as demonstrated by the ice ages.

There is an alternative theory that explains why the polar ice can shrink without the average temperature of the planet having to change. This theory is based on what the Bible tells us about creation. If our Creator is truly Almighty and desires a personal relationship with each of us as He claims, then we should expect the Bible to be consistent with unbiased scientific evidence.

Those who say that the activity of man is to blame for the shrinking polar ice are uniformitarians who assume conditions on earth have been in a steady state for millions of years. However, it is also possible that the bulk of the polar ice was formed suddenly at a catastrophic event. The shrinking polar ice would then be the result of the Second Law of Thermodynamics being played out on a global scale. The Second Law of Thermodynamics says that entropy or randomness will increase so that the energy in a closed system becomes more dispersed or less ordered over time. If the polar ice was formed suddenly, its existence is not the natural state and we should expect polar temperatures to rise as global temperatures become less polarized over time.

11.1 The Earth before Noah's Flood

The Bible describes a time when conditions on earth were very different than today. Dinosaurs roamed the planet, people lived to be hundreds of years old, and it did not rain. All this changed with a worldwide flood.

Mankind was on the earth at the same time as dinosaurs. Fossils of human and dinosaur foot prints have been found in the same rock strata in many places; one such place is on the Paluxy River about 40 miles Southwest of Fort Worth, Texas. There are a lot of theories as to what happened to the dinosaurs; Some think dinosaurs just couldn't compete with mammals, others think that the dinosaurs' lack of intelligence led to their demise, but the Bible tells us what really happened...

11.2 The Quick-Freezing of the Poles

In the beginning, God created our world out of nothing (Genesis 1:1-2). The earth was originally created with an atmospheric layer of water vapor called a firmament (Genesis 1:7). The water vapor canopy kept temperatures uniform across the planet so it did not rain (Genesis 2:5). This dense water vapor layer compressed the air beneath resulting in a higher atmospheric pressure than today. It also diffused the solar radiation so that temperatures were moderate everywhere across the globe. This facilitated the growth of more plant life than we have today resulting in higher oxygen content. Thus, the atmosphere was like a gigantic hyperbolic chamber which hospitals use to accelerate healing. This helps explain how people could live longer than they do today.

Over time, centrifugal force caused the water vapor canopy to mass over the equator making for a thinner vapor barrier at the poles. At the worldwide flood of Noah's day, most of the water in the vapor canopy precipitated down to the earth causing the vapor barrier to break up (Genesis 7:11). Since the vapor barrier was thinner at the poles, it broke up there first. The high pressure air venting through the vapor barrier at the poles caused a dramatic cooling effect, thus forming the polar ice. This is how air conditioners and refrigerators work; a rapidly expanding gas results in cooling.

After forty days of rain, the earth was covered in water (Genesis 7:19). Eventually, the flood subsided leaving conditions on earth as we know it today (Genesis 8:14).

11.3 God's Word is True

The rapid formation of polar ice is supported by evidence such as the discovery of mammoths frozen so quickly that some still had food in their mouths. Also, explorers in Antarctica routinely report seeing tropical vegetation frozen in the ice crevasses. The uniformitarian naturalists try to explain that with continent shift, but this would take too long to preserve vegetation that only grows in the tropics.

There is actually a lot of scientific evidence that the earth is not as old as evolutionists would have us believe. For example, from satellite imagery we know how much silt has been deposited in the Gulf of Mexico by the Mississippi River. We also know how much is deposited on average each year so simple math tells us how long this process has been going on. It is on the order of 5,000 years, not the multi-millions of years that evolutionists have to believe to give their theory any hope of working. Naturalists have to ignore such data or come up with convoluted theories to make the data fit their worldview. In this case, they say the impact of civilization has changed the rate of silt being deposited. But this does not hold water because human activities have actually reduced the amount of silt washed down the Mississippi River.

The conventional wisdom is that rock dating proves the earth to be multi-millions of years old but it is important to understand how rock dating works. All rock dating techniques make assumptions as to how much radioactive material was originally in rocks. And no one knows what this is! Rock dating has declared lava rocks to be millions of years old in cases where their age is known to be only a 100 years old from the history of the volcano eruption that formed them.

Carbon-14 dating is limited to once-living matter but is significantly more reliable than rock dating. No assumptions need to be made because the amount of Carbon-14 originally in the matter is known from living organisms. Fossil fuels are the oldest once-living matter on earth. Carbon-14 dating reveals oil and coal to be only tens of thousands of years old, several orders of magnitude less than the multi-millions of years as evolutionists would have us believe.

Thus we need to question the conventional wisdom about global warming and our origins as well. These are important issues that have far-reaching spiritual implications.

11.4 Global Warming Hysteria

There will be signs in the sun, moon and stars. On the earth, nations
will be in anguish and perplexity at the roaring and tossing of the sea.
Men will faint from terror, apprehensive of what is coming on the world.
(Luke 21:25-26, NIV)

The hysteria over global warming is a sign we are near the return of Christ. Government leaders have taken advantage of the fear of what is coming to create a crisis that must be addressed now. They are using the controversial threat of something that could happen in the future to cause people to accept unpleasant changes today.

The "settled science" of global warming has gotten so politically correct that it has become a powerful religion. Global warming skeptics are ostracized as being anti-science. Humanists who say they only want to act in the best interests of mankind would impose draconian measures on people for the sake of future generations. They are not really acting in the best interests of people; they are imposing their religion on others.

Some radical environmentalists even view people as a blight on the planet that is killing "Mother Earth." And in extreme cases, militant environmentalists don't think a nuclear war would be such a bad thing; it would help to cull the population which they think would reduce global warming. No-doubt militant environmentalists secretly cheer on terrorists in their quest for WMDs.

11.5 Biblical Global Warming

The present heavens and earth are reserved for fire, being kept for the day

of judgment and destruction of ungodly men. (2 Peter 3:7, NIV)
The Bible says the earth will indeed experience global warming. Those with the global warming religion should fear what is coming because any of today's mild global warming pales before the real global warming that God will send on the earth at the end of the Millennial Kingdom. This ultimate global warming is indeed caused by mankind as a consequence for turning away from God, not due to producing carbon dioxide.

11.6 Man Caused Global Warming

He is before all things, and in Him all things hold together.
(Colossians 1:17, NIV)
God is in control of our climate. It is arrogant to think that mankind is so powerful that we can change the climate of the earth. Humanists have a uniformitarian view of the world, *"all things continue as they were from the beginning of creation"* (2 Peter 3:4). Humanists don't bother to consider that the ice ages prove we can have fluctuations in climate not caused by man. So when the climate appears to be changing they think the activities of mankind must surely behind it. They have no concept of a personal God who intervenes in the affairs of man. It doesn't even cross their minds that God is behind the record weather events serving His purpose to give His faithful yet another sign that Jesus will soon return. The perception of changing climate also gives humanists one more reason to move toward a global government.

11.7 Global Warming Agenda

All the world marveled and followed the beast (Revelation 13:3)
The Bible says that all the world will come together to follow the Antichrist. Global warming is being used to push the world toward a global government. Global problems require global solutions so fixing climate change is a greater task than any one nation can take on by itself. Thus all nations must set aside their sovereignty in the interests of the greater good. This means that rich nations like the U.S. will need to give up some of its economic power in the interest of "fairness" to be more of a team player in the world's community of nations. Fixing global warming will be a tool used to "spread the wealth around" on a global scale. Ultimately such control over market economies will require a totalitarian global government to administer it, just in time for the Antichrist to take power. The secret global

warming agenda is all about taxing progress and taking freedom away from the public.

11.8 Biblical Environmentalism

God blessed them and said to them, "Be fruitful and increase in number; fill the earth and subdue it. Rule over the fish of the sea and the birds of the air and over every living creature that moves on the ground."
(Genesis 1:28, NIV)

Global warming advocates often accuse those with a biblical world-view as being anti-environmentalists. That could not be further from the truth. God commanded us to be good stewards of the earth and that means using the available resources wisely. Polluting the environment is not good stewardship of the earth. The issue really is whether carbon dioxide is pollution. People and animals exhale carbon dioxide with every breath we take. Are we polluting by breathing? Militant environmentalists would have us think so. Vegetation requires carbon dioxide to grow and the oxygen we need to breathe is given off the in the process. Plants will grow faster and bigger if more carbon dioxide is available to them. God has made our biosphere self-correcting so the atmosphere can not have too much carbon dioxide.

11.9 Global Warming Dogma

Come, let us build ourselves a city, with a tower that reaches to the heavens, so that we may make a name for ourselves (Genesis 11:4, NIV)

Being on the politically correct side of the global warming issue has become a litmus test for where a person stands on a whole collection of humanist issues. Solving the great global warming threat has become so urgent because it will be a great monument to human achievement. As people thought they could reach God at the Tower of Babel by coming together to pool their efforts, people today think they can achieve their own deliverance from the ravages of global warming by collective action. The hysteria over global warming is being whipped up to a religious fervor. Indeed the idea that mankind is causing global warming is considered to be a fundamental truth that can not be contradicted.

11.10 Bad Weather Forecasts

In their hearts humans plan their course, but the Lord establishes their steps.
(Proverbs 16:9, NIV)

You'd think in this enlightened age with computer models forecasting doom decades from now if we don't cut back our carbon emissions, that we could at least get a 24-hour forecast right. The global warming faithful are quick to say that climate is not weather as if that gives them license to ignore the limitations of computer models. But the problem is global warming proponents base their entire argument of the doom to come on computer models. As anyone who has worked with computer models know, they are only as good as the information and algorithms they are given.

The computer models used to predict the weather are simpler than those being used to predict the climate. Global warming proponents claim that their more complex climate models are better than those used for predicting the weather so we should trust them. They don't even recognize this debased logic. If you can't get the simple right, why should we trust you with the more complex? Indeed this problem with modeling has led to "Bonini's Paradox" which explains the challenges of simulations that fully represent complex systems. French philosopher Paul Valéry effectively summarized this paradox in advance when he said, "Everything simple is false. Everything which is complex is unusable" (Notre destin et les lettres, 1937).

Trust in God, not computer models generated by scientists seeking funding from the government in support of an agenda.

11.11 Wildfires

The first angel sounded: And hail and fire followed, mingled with blood, and they were thrown to the earth. And a third of the trees were burned up, and all green grass was burned up. (Revelation 8:7)

Wildfires are scary things for homeowners in rural areas. But they do serve to remind us of the even more terrible fires that will happen during the Tribulation when all the grass and a third the trees will be consumed. Followers of Christ can take comfort from knowing that the Rapture will happen prior to the Tribulation so we don't have to experience the worst of the wildfires that are coming.

11.12 Tornados

Behold, disaster shall go forth from nation to nation, and a great whirlwind
shall be raised up from the farthest parts of the earth (Jeremiah 25:32)

Tornados cause terrible destruction. When we hear of one, it should remind us of an even more terrible time of destruction that will occur during the Tribulation. As tornados are an act of God, the Tribulation will be a great pouring out of God's wrath from the pent-up consequences for mankind turning away from the Creator. But good things will come from the Tribulation; it culminates in Jesus Christ returning to the earth to begin His Millennial Reign.

11.13 Great Storms

Behold, the Lord has a mighty and strong one, like a tempest of hail
and a destroying storm, like a flood of mighty waters overflowing,
who will bring them down to the earth with His hand (Isaiah 28:2)

When we see great storms, we witness the power of God. We often wonder why God brought such destruction upon us with a terrible storm but He may have sent it just to reset our priorities and refocus our attention on Him. As painful as a disaster from a great storm may be, God can use such an event for a greater good such as helping people grow closer to Him (Romans 8:28).

12 TECHNOLOGY

Technology is a gift from God as a reward for studying the creation to learn more about our Creator. Proof is given in this chapter for the scientific accuracy of the Bible and various theories offering alternative explanations to the biblical account of creation are discussed. Multiple examples are given showing that the Bible has a lot to say about the state of our technology in the time-frame of the Lord's return.

God brought order out of chaos in the creation. This demonstrated that creating new things from the stuff of the earth is inherently good (Genesis 1:1, 2, 31). The creativity of God didn't end with the creation, it is part of His nature: *"Jesus Christ is the same yesterday and today and forever"* (Hebrews 13:8). God is a maker and He made us, His image-bearers (Genesis 1:27), to also be makers commanding us to, *"Rule over the fish of the sea and the birds of the air and over every living creature that moves on the ground"* (Genesis 1:28, NIV). Bringing order to God's creation by making things is part of ruling over it. We know we are fulfilling our purpose when we derive satisfaction from exercising our creativity as we produce useful things.

The Creator sees our creations as an extension of His own work (see Jeremiah 22:6). God cares about the details of what we build; He gave detailed instructions for building Noah's ark, the tabernacle and temple. He gifts us with the special *"skill, ability and knowledge"* we need to be creative (Exodus 31:3, NIV). Since we have gifts from God, He wants us to use them (Romans 12:6).

12.1 Faith Gave Birth to Science

Secular humanists, atheists and other naturalists try to convince us that science is not compatible with faith in Christ. But God told us, *"Come now, let us reason together"* (Isaiah 1:18). God does not call us to blind faith; He gave us a capacity to use logic for discerning the truth. Our faith is reasonable because there is sufficient evidence that reinforces it for those who really want to know the truth.

Indeed, the scientific method itself was developed by Renaissance-era Christian scientists who realized that since our Creator is the God of order, we can learn more about Him by studying His creation; *"Since the creation of the world God's invisible qualities—his eternal power and divine nature—have been clearly seen, being understood from what has been made"* (Romans 1:20, NIV). Originally, the motivation for doing science was to glorify God by getting to know Him through studying the creation. The religious motivation of the first scientists is why science became a self-sustaining enterprise only in the Christian West; *"to search out a matter is the glory of kings"* (Proverbs 25:2, NIV)

God created for us a world with universal laws which facilitates our learning about the creation. For example, the motion of the moon can be explained by a study of gravitation on earth. Being in the image of God gives people the capacity to share in His rationality. Thus the more we exercise our thinking capacity to know God better and apply this knowledge, the more like Him we will be. Doing this pleases our Lord: *"Love the Lord your God with all your heart and with all your soul and with all your mind. This is the first and greatest commandment"* (Matthew 22:37-38, NIV).

Another reason Christian scientists were motivated to apply their knowledge is the idea that working to improve mankind's condition results in personal rewards in an eternally lasting way (Matthew 6:20). This understanding is inherent in a biblical worldview where what really happened in the beginning and what will happen at the end of the world is known. Secular humanists try to claim that it is they who are more motivated to improve mankind's condition but if there is no life after death, there is no lasting personal benefit to good works. This is certainly seen in charitable giving which is substantially greater among born again Christians than the general population on a per-capita basis. Also, seeing the universe as having endless historical cycles ultimately results in hopelessness or complacency in humanists who honestly consider their fate.

Naturalists scoff at Christian beliefs saying there is no scientific evidence that what the Bible claims is true. But science only has value in the material world and there is more than this material world. The evidence for that truth can be found by those who allow themselves to honestly seek it without bias (Matthew 7:7). For example, there really have been Bible prophecies that have been fulfilled in history and this is powerful evidence for the supernatural intervention of God in our world. Helping others to consider the evidence of fulfilled prophecy could be what enables them to believe the Bible really is the supernatural Word of God.

12.2 Scientific Accuracy of Bible

The entirety of Your word is truth, and every one of Your righteous judgments endures forever (Psalm 119:160)

Many people will be surprised to learn that the Bible is scientifically accurate. But you'd expect that to be the case if the Bible is the Word of God as it claims. The following are some examples that may be used to help people see that the Bible has always been ahead of the times:

12.3 Spherical Earth

It is He who sits above the circle of the earth (Isaiah 40:22)

Contrary to the conventional wisdom, nowhere does the Bible say the earth is flat. There is a reference to the *"four corners of the earth"* (Isaiah 7:12, Revelation 7:1) but in context this is referring to the four cardinal directions. Taking the Bible out of context is a frequent strategy of people seeking to discredit it. The idea that the earth was flat came from Greek mythology and is not a biblical worldview. The Bible says the earth is a sphere which gave the explorer Columbus his inspiration and motivation to set out from Europe to find another way to India.

12.4 Earth in Space

He hangs the earth on nothing (Job 26:7)

The Bible says that God suspended the earth in space. This is contrary to mankind's conventional wisdom for most of history. The first scientist having this biblical understanding of the earth would appear to be Copernicus around 1500. Having a biblical worldview frees us from the errors inherent in mere human reasoning.

12.5 Vast Universe

"Do I not fill heaven and earth?" says the LORD. (Jeremiah 23:24)
God is Almighty enough to have created an enormous universe. We are just now beginning to understand how big. The sun is 93 million miles away from earth, 8.3 minutes away at the speed of light and 163 years at 65 miles per hour. The most remote known satellite of the sun, Pluto is 3.7 billion miles from the sun, 5.5 hours at the speed of light and 6,500 years away at 65 miles per hour. The closest star to the sun, Alpha Centauri is ~25 trillion miles away, 4.3 light-years and 44.5 million years away at 65 miles per hour. The closest galaxy, Andromeda is ~2.6 million light-years away and the furthest known galaxy is 13.2 billion light-years away.

12.6 Star Count

I will make the descendants of David my servant and the Levites who minister before me as countless as the stars in the sky (Jeremiah 33:22, NIV)
Before telescopes, star gazers estimated there had to be on the order of 6,000 stars in the sky. Once the telescope was invented, the Prussian astronomer Friedrich Argelander began counting stars and cataloged over 458,000 of them in the Northern Hemisphere from his vantage point in Germany. Today, we know from the work of the Hubble Space Telescope that there are on the order of 100 billion stars in our galaxy alone. If we counted these stars at one star per second, it would take over 3000 years. And that is just our galaxy; the Hubble Telescope also revealed that there are about 100 billion galaxies in the universe.

While our vast universe is incomprehensible in human terms, it is not to God. *"Lift up your eyes on high, and see who has created these things, who brings out their host by number; he calls them all by name"* (Isaiah 40:26). God has a name for each of the ten thousand trillion stars in the universe. Amazing!

12.7 Diverse Celestial Bodies

There is one glory of the sun, another glory of the moon, and another glory of the stars; for one star differs from another star in glory.
(1 Corinthians 15:41)
It is now known that there is incredible variety among the stars. There are red giants, white dwarfs, neutron stars, pulsar Cepheid

variables, and on and on it goes with more discoveries by astronomers all the time.

12.8 Big Bang Problems

The heavens declare the glory of God; and the firmament shows
His handiwork. (Psalm 19:1)

If a "Big Bang" is what distributed all the matter in the universe, we would expect there to be a fairly uniform distribution of matter throughout the universe. This is what happens when a symmetrical bomb explodes. And the super dense black hole singularity event proposed by Big Bang theorists would have to by definition be symmetrical. But this is not what astronomers have discovered. The universe has complex structures of galaxies that defy any homogenous distribution of matter.

One discovery that could be used to support the Big Bang Theory's symmetrical expectation for matter in the universe is the uniform distribution of background radiation. The problem is that this is in stark contrast to the uneven distribution of matter in the universe. So Big Bang theorists have had to come up with the theories of mysterious dark matter and dark energy in a attempt to explain this discrepancy. It is too bad they don't apply Occam's Razor and embrace the far simpler explanation of the creation account in Genesis.

12.9 Redshift

Thus says God the LORD, who created the heavens and stretched them out
(Isaiah 42:5)

Redshift is an application of the Doppler effect applied to light. If the light spectrum of a distant light source shifts to the blue end of the spectrum over time, the object is moving toward the observer, if the shift is toward the red, the light source is moving away. Astronomers have used redshift to determine that the universe's galaxies are accelerating apart. This is inconsistent with the naturalist Big Bang Theory which would expect deceleration due to gravitational forces. So scientists have had to explain the expansion of the galaxies with their theories of dark matter and the curvature of space. The more we learn about the universe, the more the biblical account is supported.

12.10 Fully Formed Galaxies

Then God said, "Let there be light"; and there was light. (Genesis 1:3)

Another problem for the Big Bang theorists is that the most distant galaxies at thirteen billion light-years away look the same as the near galaxies. Given the limitation of the speed of light, what we see from earth should be what the distant galaxies looked like thirteen billion years ago. So if the universe is thirteen billion years old, we should expect the distant galaxies to be just unformed gas clouds, not fully formed galaxies. God created the universe fully mature just as Adam and Eve were created as mature adults. (The chicken really did come before the egg.) The light from the distant galaxies did not take thirteen billion light-years to reach the earth; God spoke the completed light-beams into existence instantly (Genesis 1:3). Yes, our Creator-God is that powerful!

12.11 Earth-Centered Universe

Now the dwelling of God is with men, and He will live with them.
(Revelation 21:3, NIV)

The earth is unique because it is the home of people God created in His image (Genesis 1:26-27). And furthermore, God will reside with mankind on the new earth for eternity (Revelation 22:5). The idea that the earth is special in God's universe is supported by discoveries of astronomers indicating that it has to be near the center of the universe.

Redshifts reveal that galaxies are accelerating away from us in the same way, in all directions. This would not be the case if the earth was located just randomly amongst the exploding matter of the universe as the Big Bang Theory would suggest.

Another observation supporting the idea the earth has to be near the center of the universe is that the cosmic microwave background radiation comes to us very uniformly from all directions. This would not be the case if the earth was anywhere else but the center of all the stars which are the source of the background radiation.

As astronomers have catalogued the location of the galaxies of the universe, it has become apparent that they seem to be in quantized distances from the Milky Way. The galaxies of the universe appear to be arrayed in shells about a million light years apart. Thus earth must be within 100,000 light-years from the center of galaxy shells or they would not appear this way.

The Pioneer 10 and Pioneer 11 spacecrafts have gone further from earth than any other. Both Pioneer spacecrafts are leaving the

Solar System with an escape velocity that is slowing due to the Sun's gravity. But the observed trajectory of the spacecrafts have shown that they are slowing more than expected. This anomaly has perplexed cosmologists who have come up with various theories to explain it. But this anomaly is actually best explained by the essentials of creationist cosmology with a bounded universe and a cosmic center of mass. So this is yet more evidence that our Solar System is near the center of the universe.

12.12 Occam's Razor

As the serpent deceived Eve by his craftiness, so your minds may be corrupted from the simplicity that is in Christ (2 Corinthians 11:3)

Secular cosmologists have had to invent many convoluted theories to explain observations of our universe. The Big Bang Theory was originally devised to support the idea that the earth is in no special place in the universe. The Copernican principle, which holds that the universe has no edge and no center requires another theory, dark energy to work. And thus over 75% of the energy density of the universe has to exist as dark energy from dark matter. Dark energy, also known as quintessence, springs from the physics of extra dimensions which has been derived from string theory. The problem of all galaxies expanding away from the earth has resulted in another theory of the curvature of space. This theory puts all matter on the surface of an expanding balloon; thus expansion away may be observed from all perspectives.

All these complex theories do not pass Occam's razor. This principle helps us select the most plausible of competing hypotheses based on the one with the simplest explanation. The Genesis account of creation is the simplest explanation thus it has to be considered the most plausible. It is amazing the convoluted theories people develop just to deny the obvious.

12.13 First Law of Thermodynamics

The heavens and the earth which are now preserved by the same word (2 Peter 3:7)

God created the universe to conform to principles that we can discover. This idea led to one of the more fundamental principles in physics: the First Law of Thermodynamics discovered in 1850 addresses the conservation of matter and energy in a closed system. If

God didn't create order for the universe, our discoveries would be worthless because they wouldn't work consistently everywhere, every time.

12.14 Second Law of Thermodynamics

The creation itself also will be delivered from the bondage of corruption
(Romans 8:21)

The Second Law of Thermodynamics discovered in 1850 says that entropy (increasing randomness) is the natural order of matter and energy. This law which explains why iron rusts probably came about as a consequence of the original sin of Adam and Eve, see Genesis 3:17-18. The Second Law of Thermodynamics also makes it real hard to buy the theory of evolution which would have us believe that more ordered, complex molecules form spontaneously from randomized states. It just doesn't happen. And the weak claim that physical laws do not apply to biological systems is just deceptive bunk. It takes a lot of faith to believe that evolution is true.

12.15 Atmospheric Pressure

He looks to the ends of the earth, and sees under the whole heavens,
to establish a weight for the wind (Job 28:24-25)

The Bible tells us that the atmosphere has a pressure that varies. Scientists did not acknowledge this truth until Torricelli discovered barometric pressure in 1643. A great way to be ahead of the times is to study the Bible.

12.16 Continental Drift

Peleg... in his days the earth was divided. (Genesis 10:25)

Scientists now believe that all continents of the earth were once connected. It is easy to see from the shape of the Eastern coast of South America how it one-time fit into the Western coast of Africa. The Bible has told us from ancient times what scientists have only recently concluded.

12.17 Sea Currents

The fish of the sea that pass through the paths of the seas (Psalm 8:8)

The fact that the ocean has predictable currents is a biblical concept. Matthew Maury (1806-1873) was inspired by Psalm 8:4-8 to discover and chart systematic ocean currents.

12.18 Ocean Springs
Have you entered the springs of the sea? (Job 38:16)
The fact that there are deep sea springs wasn't known until 1973 when the deep diving research submarine of Project FAMOUS discovered mineralized vent springs in the Mid-Atlantic Ridge. Since then, other research dives have found more deep sea hot spring vents on the floor of other oceans.

12.19 Hydrological Cycle
All the rivers run into the sea, yet the sea is not full; to the place
from which the rivers come, there they return again
(Ecclesiastes 1:7; see also Job 36:27-28 & Amos 9:6)
The earliest literature indicating an understanding of hydrological cycle was around the Third or Fourth Century BC. Yet King Solomon was inspired by God to write about this in the Tenth Century BC.

12.20 Dinosaurs
Look now at the behemoth... he eats grass like an ox...
he moves his tail like a cedar (Job 40:15-17)
This is no West Texas cedar; cedars in the Bible refer to the cedars of Lebanon which were huge trees. Thus the *"behemoth"* of Job 40:15 must be a dinosaur. The Bible doesn't say what happened to the dinosaurs, it just correctly acknowledges they did exist. It is likely the dinosaurs lived prior to the great worldwide flood of Noah's day and were not able to survive in the world conditions after the flood.

12.21 Fossils
The world that then existed perished, being flooded with water (2 Peter 3:6)
The fact that fossils exist everywhere is evidence of the worldwide flood of Noah's day. Fossils are not being formed today. When something dies in the sea, it sinks to the ocean floor, rots, gets eaten by crabs and is dispersed by the currents. It takes a catastrophic event to cause massive silt layers to wash over living organisms to form a fossil. Thus the existence of fossils is best explained by the cataclysm of the flood.

12.22 Circumcision

He who is eight days old among you shall be circumcised,
every male child in your generations (Genesis 17:12)

God's law protected people from health problems they did not understand. Circumcision which served to set Jews apart also reduced the risk of urinary tract infections along with some sexually transmitted diseases, penile cancer in men and cervical cancer in women. Regarding the timing of circumcision, it is now known that it takes five to seven days for bacteria in the newborn male's intestinal tract to produce sufficient vitamin K which is required for the liver to produce the prothrombin necessary for blood clotting.

12.23 Infectious Diseases

This is the law when a man dies in a tent: All who come into the tent
and all who are in the tent shall be unclean seven days (Numbers 19:14)

It was not until the 20th Century that medical science came to understand that most diseases are caused by infection of microscopic organisms. The Prophet Moses was inspired by God to write this law in about 1430 BC.

12.24 Trichinosis

The swine is unclean for you… you shall not eat their flesh
or touch their dead carcasses (Genesis 17:12)

Pigs are now known to be carriers of parasites that cause trichinosis and tumors in humans if the meat is not cooked thoroughly. This was more of a problem in ancient times before ovens were widely used for cooking meat.

12.25 Toxic Mold

If the plague has spread on the walls of the house… take away
the stones in which is the plague, and they shall cast them into
an unclean place outside the city. (Leviticus 14:39-40)

The recognition that mildew causes a myriad of health problems was not taken seriously until recently. Yet God inspired the Prophet Moses to record this law in about 1430 BC.

12.26 DNA

God hath made of one blood all nations of men for to dwell
on all the face of the earth (Acts 17:26)

From a modern study of DNA, we now know that all races descended from the same ancestral parents, just as the Bible says. If people are the product of blind natural processes as the theory of evolution would have us believe, the races could have come from multiple parental sources. This is why the Nazis pursued eugenics thinking their race was superior to others. The Bible reveals that the different races came about as the gene pool became divided due to God causing people to be dispersed with different languages at the Tower of Babel (Genesis 11:1-9).

12.27 Anthropic Principle

The philosophic anthropic principle has resulted from discoveries revealing that the physical universe appears to have been designed for life. Naturalists dismiss this idea saying these discoveries are just coincidences; that these conditions just happened to be what life requires. But such discoveries constitute powerful scientific evidence for design in creation supporting the biblical worldview that God created the universe. The following are some of the more interesting discoveries that led to the anthropic principle:

- **Proton Mass** – if the mass of a proton were increased by just 0.2%, then the proton would be unstable quickly decaying to a neutron, positron, and neutrino. This would destroy all hydrogen atoms which are critical for life.
- **Gravitational Force** – the gravitational force between celestial objects is inversely proportional to the square of the separation distance with a factor of 2.00000 to five decimal places. This kind of accuracy has to be by design, it is no accident.
- **Electrical Charge Force** – the force between electrical charges is the inverse square of the distance between the charges with an astonishingly accurate factor of 2.000000000000000 (16 decimal places).
- **Earth's Magnetic Field** – if the magnetic field of the earth was much weaker, there'd be too much cosmic radiation for life; if much stronger, there would be terrible electromagnetic storms.
- **Earth's Distance from the Sun** – the earth's location in the Solar System is critical: if it was further from the sun, our planet's water would freeze; if it was closer the earth's water would boil off.

- **Earth's Place in the Galaxy** – if the earth was in the center of the Milky Way, there would be too much cosmic radiation for life; if too far away, we would not have enough heavy elements on earth to support life.
- **Solar Spectrum** – if the color of our sun was much redder or bluer, the photosynthesis that is critical for life on earth would not work.

Humanists have had to come up with various theories attempting to make sense of the Anthropic Principle within their naturalistic worldview. The following are summaries of the seven explanations for the Anthropic Principle as given in Paul Davies' book, "The Goldilocks Enigma" (2006):

1. **The absurd universe** – Our universe just happens to be the way it is. Humanists dismiss all manner of phenomena providing evidence of design declaring it to be mere coincidence.
2. **The unique universe** – There is a deep underlying unity in physics necessitating the universe being the way it is (Theory of Everything). Of course the universe is unique because God created it that way.
3. **The multiverse** – Multiple universes exist with all the permutations of characteristics that allow us to exist. Thus we are just "lucky" to be in the right universe to support life. What a coincidence!
4. **The life principle** – There is an underlying principle that constrains the universe to evolve towards life and mind. Indeed, because God created the universe that way.
5. **The self-explaining universe** – Perhaps only universes with a capacity for consciousness can exist. So is there any sound if a tree falls in the forest and there is no one around to hear it? What idiocy.
6. **The fake universe** – We live inside a virtual reality simulation. This theory probably inspired the Matrix movies. If we live in a simulation, it sure is realistic; people still look for traffic before they cross the street.
7. **Creationism** – A creator designed the universe with the purpose of supporting life as we know it. This is the only explanation of the Anthropic Principle that makes sense.

12.28 Creation Science

For since the creation of the world His invisible attributes are clearly seen, being understood by the things that are made, even His eternal power and Godhead, so that they are without excuse (Romans 1:20)

It is inherently obvious to all that if there is a creation, there must have been a Creator. The more we learn of the universe, the more we see design and evidence that supports the Genesis account of creation. People who deny this insisting on a naturalistic explanation of everything really don't want to admit accountability to the Creator-God. They are denying reality which is not a healthy condition to be in because it has eternal ramifications.

This life is a test to see who will willingly embrace their Creator. Those who reject Christ have decided to live their life separate from their Creator. They will get the desire of their hearts but it will not be what they think. God made us to have a relationship with Him (1 Corinthians 1:9); it will be pure hell to spend eternity separated from Him.

12.29 Technology Trends

The prophetic role of technology has not been apparent for most of human history. This is something that has only become significant fairly recently due to the exponential growth of technological developments. The following are some trends we see in technology which have prophetic implications:

12.30 Antichrist Technology

Come, let us build ourselves a city, with a tower that reaches to the heavens, so that we may make a name for ourselves and not be scattered over the face of the whole earth. (Genesis 11:3-4, NIV)

Technology is a gift of God but it can be a problem if it is used to diminish God's glory or to resist His will. This is what happened at the Tower of Babel. An increasing trend in science today is trying to prove that the naturalist worldview is superior to the biblical worldview. The no-God-required theory of evolution has become so pervasive that it is now more a religion than science because of the faith required to embrace it. And so much of science today has become tainted with politically correct agendas. Collaborating in science to oppose God will have consequences as it did at the Tower of Babel.

12.31 Technology Worship
He shall honor a god of fortresses (Daniel 11:38)
During the Tribulation, the Antichrist will treat technology as a god. The Prophet Daniel's *"god of fortresses"* refers to the use of technology to keep a city safe. As they used walls, towers, moats, and gates in ancient times to protect a city, we also have become dependant on our technology for security. This makes an idol of technology; looking to technology for deliverance, our creation rather than the Creator.

12.32 True Security
Unless the LORD builds the house, they labor in vain who build it;
unless the LORD guards the city, the watchman stays awake in vain
(Psalm 127:1)
We can trust in our technology to warn us and prevail against threats to our nation all we want, but God is in control and His protection is vitally important. If we forget that and turn away from God to depend on our technology, we put ourselves at risk. God will send us a reminder that we need to turn back to Him. That is what the 9/11/2001 attack on America should have done. Churches had huge crowds following this event for a while but it wasn't long before we reverted back to business as usual. Given the trend of our culture away from God, it is just a matter of time until we will be reminded of the need for God's protection yet again.

12.33 Failure of Technology
Bel is shamed. Merodach is broken in pieces; her idols are humiliated,
her images are broken in pieces (Jeremiah 50:2)
Technology has become a modern day idol; people count on technology to deliver them from everything that afflicts us. So when technology fails them, they are completely at a loss in knowing what to do. God allows technology to fail as a reminder that we should not depend on it but on Him instead. Technology is a great blessing that improves the human condition but we should not allow it to replace God in our lives.

12.34 Technological Signs

When the fullness of the time had come, God sent forth His Son
(Galatians 4:4)

The Messiah first came to earth when the state of technology had reached the point where dissemination of the gospel was possible. The Greek language was in wide use having been established as the language of commerce and Roman roads had been built to facilitate command and control over civilization. Both were necessary to get the good news of Jesus out to the world. Likewise, technology must be in a certain state to fulfill prophecies when the Lord returns. God could and will fulfill many of the prophecies through supernatural means but more often He chooses to work through natural means so that only the spiritually discerning will recognize the significance of what is happening. That is why Jesus often spoke in parables; *"Therefore I speak to them in parables, because seeing they do not see, and hearing they do not hear, nor do they understand"* (Matthew 13:13). Certainly miracles are generally only recognized by God's faithful since, *"we walk by faith, not by sight"* (2 Corinthians 5:7).

12.35 Technological Significance

You know how to discern the face of the sky, but you cannot discern the signs of the times. (Matthew 16:3)

Technology is a sign of the times. As we see technologies that God may use to fulfill prophecies, we know that the return of Christ is near.

12.36 Technology Revelations

Go your way, Daniel, because the words are closed up and sealed until the time of the end (Daniel 12:9, NIV)

As we get closer to the return of Christ, we can expect to better understand how God is going to fulfill the prophecies. In modern times, we can now see how many prophecies previously assumed to be fulfilled by supernatural means may now be fulfilled naturally.

12.37 Internet, Exploding Knowledge

Seal the book until the time of the end; many shall run to and fro, and knowledge shall increase (Daniel 12:4)

In the times leading up to the return of Christ, there will be a lot of people traveling and there will be an expansion of knowledge. This growth of knowledge pertains to both understanding in general and a better understanding of Bible prophecy in particular. General knowledge has grown exponentially with the Internet which puts an incredible wealth of information at the fingertips. Since God helps us to know Him better through progressive illumination, the fact that we better understand the Bible today than when it was written is to be expected.

12.38 Traveling

Seal the book until the time of the end; many shall run to and fro
(Daniel 12:4)

In the time-frame of Jesus returning, traveling will be easier and better through technological developments. It is interesting to note that throughout human history, people could only travel as fast as a horse could gallop, about 15 MPH. In the Twentieth Century this changed with the advent of the automobile and airplane. Now it is routine for the average person to travel daily at 70 MPH and even 500 MPH when they fly.

12.39 Automobiles

The chariots come with flaming torches in the day of his preparation, and the spears are brandished. The chariots rage in the streets, they jostle one another in the broad roads; they seem like torches, they run like lightning.
(Nahum 2:3-4)

How might a prophet during ancient times describe the vision of a freeway in a modern city at night? The reference to chariots as a vehicle of war used to inflect violence on others relates to the carnage wrought by the modern automobile. Among the top ten causes of death in the U.S. are automobile accidents.

12.40 Space Travel

"Though you soar like the eagle and make your nest among the stars,
from there I will bring you down," declares the LORD. (Obadiah 4, NIV)

Only since the space program have we been able to comprehend biblical prophecies relating to mankind's efforts in the heavens. The time-frame of Obadiah 4 is given in verse 15: *"For the day of the Lord is near."*

12.41 Television

For three and a half days men from every people, tribe, language and nation will gaze on their bodies and refuse them burial. (Revelation 11:9, NIV)
During the Tribulation, the whole world will see two prophets God sends to Jerusalem to warn mankind of the judgment that is coming. No one can stop these two prophets until the Antichrist kills them. The entire world will view their bodies and their resurrection. Before the days of television and satellite communications, people just had to assume that God would enable all the world to witness this through supernatural means. We now know that they will watch it on CNN and their smart phones.

12.42 Satellite Communications

I saw another angel flying in the midst of heaven, having the everlasting gospel to preach to those who dwell on the earth (Revelation 14:6)
During the Tribulation, the gospel will be preached to the whole world by an angel in heaven. This is a fulfillment of the prophecy that, *"this gospel of the kingdom will be preached in all the world as a witness to all the nations, and then the end will come"* (Matthew 24:14). Now this will probably be fulfilled as a supernatural event but it also could be a veiled reference to satellite communications. The word "angel" literally means "messenger." Certainly the advent of communications satellites foreshadows this ultimate fulfillment of prophecy because they facilitate the gospel's broadcast to all nations even today.

12.43 RFID Mark of the Beast

He also forced everyone, small and great, rich and poor, free and slave, to receive a mark on his right hand or on his forehead, so that no one could buy or sell unless he had the mark (Revelation 13:16-17, NIV)
Before modern times is was hard to conceive how the Antichrist would be able to have control over all commerce. But with our dependence on computer technology that facilitates financial transactions, it is obvious how the beast will micromanage the economy. And the advent of rice-grain-sized radio frequency identification chips implanted under the skin provides even more insight how transactions may be controlled.

While the mark of the beast technology likely exists today, that does not mean the mark of the beast is in place yet. This will not happen until the Tribulation when the Antichrist is in power and people are required to swear allegiance to him before they are allowed to engage in commerce. Thus, the Church should never have to worry about the mark of the beast.

12.44 Robotics, Artificial Intelligence

He was granted power to give breath to the image of the beast, that the image of the beast should both speak and cause as many as would not worship the image of the beast to be killed. (Revelation 13:15)

Since the Antichrist will not be omniscient as God, technology will be employed to take up the slack. There will be many images of the beast used to make sure people are complying with his will. In times past believers would just have to think the image of the beast needed demonic forces to work. But in modern times, technology has advanced to the point where robots duplicate many human capabilities. Automation has improved manufacturing but will be used by the Antichrist to facilitate his controlling people. Today we have machine vision that can read people's facial expressions, body language and gestures. Artificial intelligence makes decisions without the need for human involvement.

During the Tribulation to come, those who "rage against the machine" will be hunted down and killed as an enemy of society. For all who fear the coming tyranny of the machines, the best way to do that is to escape the Tribulation by being a follower of Christ before this current Church Age comes to its dramatic end.

12.45 Nuclear Weapons

If those days had not been cut short, no one would survive, but for the sake of the elect those days will be shortened. (Matthew 24:22, NIV)

It has only been since the late 1940's that it is possible to comprehend weapons that could annihilate all life on earth. Of all the ways known for people to die, only nuclear weapons could cause the death described in Zechariah 14:12: *"their flesh shall dissolve while they stand on their feet, their eyes shall dissolve in their sockets, and their tongues shall dissolve in their mouths."*

12.46 Transhumanism

The serpent said to the woman, "You will not surely die." (Genesis 3:4)

Transhumanists want people to pursue becoming "beyond human." People with this vision believe technology will help mankind make the next evolutionary leap beyond our current human condition. They believe technology will enable people to live significantly longer lives and eventually not cease to exist. It includes the idea that computers will become advanced enough that our minds could be downloaded into them and thus not be subject to a body that will grow old and die.

Transhumanism is just one more facet of rejecting God's provision for mankind as part of a humanist worldview. It is interesting that we are living in a time that technology is advanced enough that people can think transhumanism is possible. This then makes the advanced state of our technology one more sign that we are close to the return of Christ. God is jealous (Exodus 20:5) and will have to respond to people raising up such a blatant idol to Him as He did at the Tower of Babel (Genesis 11:1-9).

12.47 Latest Health Discovery

We will no longer be infants, tossed back and forth by the waves, and blown here and there by every wind of teaching and by the cunning and craftiness of men in their deceitful scheming (Ephesians 4:14, NIV)

It is pretty much a waste of time making lifestyle changes due to the latest health news. How many times have you changed what you eat due to some "discovery" reported in the health news only to be contradicted by some later report? People with ulterior motives are "cooking" the results of their "scientific" research to influence behavior in which they have a vested interest. You can provide statistical "evidence" for anything you want just by manipulating sample groups and sizes. This is why poll results should also be taken with a grain of salt because there is usually an agenda being promoted. Great discernment is called for today to keep from being blown about by every wind of teaching by people with deceitful scheming. The Bible warns us to be on our guard in the face of people who seek to deceive us for gain.

12.48 Politically Correct Food

The Spirit expressly says that in latter times some will depart from the faith, giving heed to deceiving spirits and doctrines of demons, ...commanding to abstain from foods which God created to be received with thanksgiving (1 Timothy 4:1-3)

Classifying some foods as good and others as bad is a sign of the times which goes along with rejecting God. People were vegetarians in the time before Noah's flood but God told us we needed to eat meat after the flood. The Fall resulted in the nutritional value of vegetables to not be as good so eating meat is necessary for protein. Thus, we shouldn't worry about what kinds of meat we eat due to the promise that God gave us in Genesis 9:3, *"everything that lives and moves will be food for you."* And when we do eat something questionable, we should find the words of Jesus to be comforting: *"What goes into a man's mouth does not make him "unclean," but what comes out of his mouth, that is what makes him 'unclean'"* (Matthew 15:11, NIV).

12.49 Discoveries Supporting Evolution

God said, "Let the land produce living creatures according to their kinds: livestock, creatures that move along the ground, and wild animals, each according to its kind." And it was so. (Genesis 1:24, NIV)

With the pervasiveness of the evolutionary worldview, the media loves to report on the latest discovery that might be an evolutionary missing link. Indeed, most people do not want to be accountable to God and thus are anxious to prove His Word to be wrong. Discovering a missing link is important to evolutionists because there is a conspicuous lack of scientific evidence for evolution. Most of the potential missing links that have been reported on have been found to be in error or even a hoax. But you'll never hear a retraction of the original story leaving the public with the idea that there is evidence for evolution. The evolutionary worldview is a powerful religion.

12.50 Potential for Extraterrestrial Life

In the beginning God created the heavens and the earth. (Genesis 1:1)

People are fascinated with the idea that there may be extraterrestrial life. The discovery of extraterrestrial life would prove the Bible wrong which represents life on earth as being unique and special. Discovering extraterrestrial life would reinforce evolution as being the source of life; if life could happen somewhere else then life is not so special on earth and God was not needed to bring it about. Mankind looks for code patterns from space with SETI (Search for Extraterrestrial Intelligence) when what they seek is right under their nose. What is DNA if not code patterns that could only have been authored by a supreme extraterrestrial intelligence, God Himself.

13 THE CULTURE

The Culture is an important indicator of the collective spiritual condition of people. This chapter contrasts the majority humanist worldview with biblical Christianity; cultural trends are discussed along with the more common moral failings. An exposition is made of 2 Timothy 3:1-7 which addresses degenerating society in the "last days." The apostasy of the current Laodicean Church Age is also discussed.

A culture war is raging around us. This provides Christians with great opportunities to help others see what the Bible says about the issues. We need to be prepared to engage in conversations on hot-button topics that are regularly in the news because this may lead to a conversation which helps people grow closer to Christ.

Our objective should not to be to win a debate but to be ready to plant a seed of biblical truth that God can use to lead people to Him. While the Bible doesn't have much impact on people if they don't regard it as the Word of God, truth does resonate and the appeal to authority outside one's own feelings is logical. Over time God can use such exposure to bear eternal fruit in a person's life.

Even if someone does not recognize the authority of the Bible, it is still beneficial to them to point out what the Bible says about contentious issues. It helps them to understand why Christians take the position they do. It also plants a "faith flag" that tells people that you are a follower of Christ. God can use these seeds of truth to turn hearts to Him; *"My Word... will not return to me empty, but will accomplish what I desire and achieve the purpose for which I sent it"* (Isaiah 55:10-11, NIV).

13.1 Worldviews

A person's worldview is the lens through which one views the world. It is the system a person settles on to fill in the gaps of information they have and thus make sense of things. People make important life decisions based on their worldview.

The term "worldview" is a euphemism for a person's religion. It is what they put their faith in and what they believe to be true. Everyone has some sort of belief system that gives them a bias. God created us to *"live by faith"* (Romans 1:17) so if we don't have faith in Him, we have to have faith in something else.

13.2 Religious Humanism

There are two basic worldviews: a biblical worldview and a humanist worldview. Most people have a humanist worldview despite the label they use to describe themselves. There are religious humanists as well as secular humanists. Religions such as Islam and Hinduism are at their core humanist religions because they believe salvation is based on one's good works (human actions). This is in sharp contrast to biblical Christianity where salvation is a function only of God's grace (Ephesians 2:8-9). Biblical Christianity is distinguished from all the worlds' religions in that salvation is the result of a personal relationship with the Savior, not anything we do ourselves. A person may claim to have a biblical worldview but taint certain aspects of their beliefs with the need to earn God's favor by good works which can only mean they are really a humanist. Salvation is by Christ alone (John 14:6).

13.3 Secular Humanism

When the term "humanism" is used, "secular humanism" is implied because it generally describes people who don't consider themselves to be religious. Indeed, some of them will even get angry if we call their humanist belief system a religion. So it is safer to refer to humanism as a worldview.

The following are key distinctions between humanism and biblical Christianity. Most of these comments apply to secular humanism; religious humanism is more similar to Christianity but with fundamental unbiblical doctrinal differences. Satan loves to copy God; *"And no wonder! For Satan himself transforms himself into an angel of light"* (2 Corinthians 11:14).

13.4 Faith

The just shall live by faith (Romans 1:17)

Humanists trust in themselves and in human institutions for their deliverance. Christians trust in God. What we ultimately need deliverance from is death and Jesus made it possible for us to have everlasting life if we trust in His provision. But our deliverance is not just in eternity, it is for the here and now, Jesus came that we may have an *"abundant life"* (John 10:10). Secular humanism is clearly deficient with either no expectation of life after death, or some vague amorphous concept of everyone going to heaven. Religious humanists are deluded into thinking their good works have earned them favor with God for salvation.

13.5 Authority

All Scripture is given by inspiration of God, and is profitable for doctrine,
for reproof, for correction, for instruction in righteousness (2 Timothy 3:16)

Among the authorities humanists recognize to obey are their own conscience and human institutions. Most would hold themselves up as their own ultimate authority; they are the captain of their own soul. Christians recognize these same authorities but those with a biblical worldview consider God's Word to be the ultimate authority in their life. When we make the Bible the ultimate authority in our life we are making God our ruler.

13.6 Salvation

For God so loved the world that He gave His only begotten Son, that whoever
believes in Him should not perish but have everlasting life (John 3:16)

Most humanists have no real hope for life after death. For those who do, they are trusting in their own good works to earn favor with God and thus merit salvation. The problem is, they don't really know how good is good enough. They don't want to face the fact that it is not possible to earn salvation because God's standard is perfection (Matthew 5:48). The Christian does not have to depend on his or her own performance for salvation because Jesus died for us (Romans 5:8).

13.7 Eternity

Father, …You loved Me before the foundation of the world (John 17:24)
The only thing eternal in the mind of the typical humanist is the matter of the universe; they are materialists. As the high priest of materialism, Carl Sagan said in his famous statement of faith, "the cosmos is all there is, was, or ever will be." There are humanists who do claim to believe in God but their view of Him is an impersonal deity who does not care or bother to intervene in the affairs of men; they are deists. Religious humanists often have a more biblical view of eternity but this is often tainted with unbiblical ideas about God and not expecting a physical resurrection. Those with a biblical view of God see Him as the Triune Godhead; the Father who sent the Son to make the way for us to spend eternity with Him and the Holy Spirit sent by the Father to be our Helper until the Son returns.

13.8 Origins

In the beginning God created the heavens and the earth (Genesis 1:1)
Humanists believe the world came into being by a "big bang" and people are just evolved animals. The reason such a belief has an appeal is that it relieves them from being accountable to the Creator. They are taking a monumental risk if they are wrong. If the Bible is true, having a humanist worldview will have severe consequences. Christians lose nothing if they are wrong. It is simply illogical to not embrace a biblical worldview. Religious humanists err by inventing their own concept of God rather than embracing the Creator's revelation of Himself.

13.9 Human nature

The heart is deceitful above all things, and desperately wicked; who can know it? (Jeremiah 17:9)
If you are not accountable to God, right and wrong is only dependant on what human authorities says it is. So humanists have no concept of sin. Believing that people are basically good gets humanists in trouble all the time. They are always being caught by surprise when others act selfishly instead of acting in the best interest of the collective. Christians recognize the basic sin nature of all people and plan for it thus making better decisions. Religious humanists have their

own invented concept of sins which they use to control and even oppress others.

13.10 Luck

I have set before you an open door, and no one can shut it (Revelation 3:8)
Humanists do not think that God cares or bothers with intervening in the affairs of people so our circumstances are just happenstance. When bad things happen, it is just bad luck. Thus humanists are slaves to the luck of the draw. Christians with a biblical worldview know that the Creator is in control; *"Are not two sparrows sold for a copper coin? And not one of them falls to the ground without your Father's will"* (Matthew 10:29). If God is in control, there are no coincidences. God often speaks to us in our circumstances. He opens and closes doors of opportunity for us for to our ultimate benefit (Romans 8:28).

13.11 Quest

Well done, good and faithful servant (Matthew 25:21)
Humanists are only motivated by what they can achieve in the world; Christians seek to please our Lord out of gratitude for what He has done for us. The humanist seeks after power, fame and money which are motivated by selfishness. Even their altruistic works ultimately have a selfish motivation to be seen as a good person and enjoy whatever worldly benefit comes from that. The pursuit of worldly treasures is shallow because it will not last; the world and everything in it is destined to be burned up (2 Peter 3:10). The Christian does good works to see God glorified knowing these also build up eternal treasure in heaven for them as a bonus.

13.12 Method

I can do all things through Christ who strengthens me (Philippians 4:13)
Secular humanists have no moral mooring, the way they pursue their goals doesn't matter, and the end justifies the means. Thus telling a lie is acceptable if it results in benefits to them that they perceive to outweigh the downside of being caught in the lie. The Christian knows that anything done outside the will of God will fail. So the more we can align our will with God, the more successful we'll be because we can access the limitless power of God.

13.13 Morality
Everyone did what was right in his own eyes (Judges 17:6)

The secular humanist doesn't have a sound moral foundation; they have a pragmatic moral foundation that changes based on circumstances. For example: from an evolutionary, survival-of-the-fittest perspective, who could really say that Hitler was wrong? Given that the victor writes the history (as they love to claim so that they may ignore history), maybe the negative spin put on the Nazis was just propaganda written by the winners? Who can really say otherwise? Humanist morality is subject to change based on human perspective and circumstances. The Christian knows that wrong is wrong because God has declared it to be.

13.14 Future Outlook
I will come again and receive you to Myself; that where I am,
there you may be also (John 14:3)

The secular humanist's vision is limited to this world. Even if they work toward something to be achieved by humanity beyond their own life, it can only be achieved in this world. Usually, what they seek after is some utopian vision of socialism or simply "survival of the species." Such goals are weak in comparison to eternity in heaven, the blessed hope that comes from a biblical worldview.

13.15 Postmodernism
Pilate said to Him, "What is truth?" (John 18:38)

Humanists in this age are moral relativists; they see truth as something that varies with perspective. Thus what is true for one person may not be for another. This means they don't believe there to be any absolute, universal truth except their belief there is no absolute, universal truth which is flawed circular reasoning. Such a worldview is a source of friction with Christians who claim to know the One who personifies Truth (John 14:6). Postmodernism prepares people mentally to embrace the deceptions of the Antichrist when truth will be what the Great Leader says it is.

13.16 Fundamentalism
Who has believed our report? And to whom has
the arm of the LORD been revealed? (Isaiah 53:1)

Bible skeptics love to malign those who take the Word of God literally. They try to lump fundamentalist Christians in with fundamentalist Islamists claiming the problem is their dogmatic beliefs. The Bible skeptics make such generalizations as if it wouldn't matter to them if they traveled on an airplane full of fundamentalist Muslims or Christians. Those who criticize fundamentalist Christians are falling victim to the irrationality that comes from postmodernism. There is truth that can be known and God has revealed it in His Word.

13.17 Cultural Trends
The following are recurring topics that often come up in the news for which having a biblical worldview would help understand their significance:

13.18 Culture War
Let both grow together until the harvest, and at the time of harvest I will say to the reapers, "First gather together the tares and bind them in bundles to burn them, but gather the wheat into my barn." (Matthew 13:30)
The escalating Culture War is a sign of the times. The voice of those who go against the will of God is getting louder trying to suppress those standing for Him. Thus the evil tare weeds are getting easier to distinguish from the wheat produced by God because both are maturing. Evil will have its day for a season but the harvest is coming when the wheat will be gathered to God and the evil weeds will be burned. It is not a good time to be mistaken for a weed.

13.19 Divorce: Devaluing Marriage
There will be terrible times in the last days.
People will be lovers of themselves (2 Timothy 3:1-2, NIV)
Growing divorce rates reveal that Western society is in terminal moral decline. The growth of single-parent families has de-stigmatized divorce and has helped to devalue marriage. This has weakened our society because the family is the fundamental building block of the nation. There are consequences from children being raised in broken homes; it is a risk factor in people turning to crime and results in dysfunctional adults causing undesirable ramifications to snowball. *"What God has joined together, let not man separate"* (Matthew 19:6).

13.20 Opposing God

"I hate divorce," says the LORD God of Israel (Malachi 2:16, NIV)

God established the institution of marriage. Denigrating marriage as God defined it opposes God. The devaluation of marriage is a symptom of people rejecting God. Divorce has become so common in our society that an increasing number of people just cohabitate not even bothering to get married. Good, long-lasting relationships between people are only possible with God's help. Our selfish nature will eventually cause the infatuation that passes for love in our society to fade. The agape sacrificial love of God is only possible in people that have an active, genuine relationship with the Savior. Jesus told us that the time-frame prior to His return would be characterized by an explosion of selfish actions (Matthew 24:12).

13.21 Child Abuse

Because lawlessness will abound, the love of many will grow cold
(Matthew 24:12)

As much as parents try to mitigate it, there is no avoiding the fact that divorce is child abuse. While such abuse is not physical, it is mental and the mental forms of abuse are often worse making a longer lasting impact. Children often think that they are to blame for the split-up of their parents despite their parents' claims to the contrary. There is increasing mental abuse even when parents stick together; while verbally berating a child has fallen out of fashion, it still goes on behind closed doors. But more frequently the abuse takes the form of just ignoring the child with TV babysitters, letting them obsess on video games, and not disciplining them at all. Since love is growing cold in this Age, there is an increasing incidence of the more traditional forms of physical abuse as well. The more we see child abuse, the more we know this world sorely needs the Lord to return.

13.22 Divorce is a Sign of the Times

I will send you the prophet Elijah before that great and dreadful day of
the LORD comes. He will turn the hearts of the fathers to their children,
and the hearts of the children to their fathers (Malachi 4:5-6, NIV)

God told us that families would be deteriorating in the time-frame of the Messiah coming. Among the bitter fruit of the selfishness that causes divorce is that children return this lack of love in kind. Selfishness will grow so that people will stop loving their children by denying them two parents and not investing their time in them. Children see through this lack of loving respect and return this learned behavior by not respecting their parents' authority. Ultimately they are rejecting God's authority because all authority is from Him.

So prior to Jesus returning, we can expect to have parents not loving their children as well as children not loving their parents. Not only is our society characterized by this today, it is a trend that is growing. God will send His prophet Elijah ahead of Jesus returning to remind people of the need to love one another. There is little doubt that Elijah is one of the two *"witnesses"* of Revelation 11:3-12 who God sends to preach in Jerusalem during the Tribulation.

13.23 Hope for the Divorced

We know that all things work together for good to those who love God, to those who are the called according to His purpose. (Romans 8:28)

There is hope for those affected by divorce. Jesus can use even our divorce pain to serve His purpose. While we may not realize in this life why God is allowing us to go through our circumstances, we will certainly see in eternity how He used our situation to craft us into the person He wants us to be. This may be cold comfort in the here and now but it is something we can build on with God's help. Anything that drives us closer to God has value.

13.24 Degenerating Society Trend

Because lawlessness will abound, the love of many will grow cold (Matthew 24:12)

The morality of our culture will continue to degenerate as a symptom of people turning away from God. The lack of love for one another and growing lawlessness in our society is a consequence of God giving us over to ourselves. It is a sign of God's coming wrath. As bad is it is now, it will continue to get worse and peak during the Tribulation.

13.25 Humanist Optimism

For when they say, "Peace and safety!" then sudden destruction comes upon them, as labor pains upon a pregnant woman. And they shall not escape. (1 Thessalonians 5:3)

The idea that the world is getting better is characteristic of humanists. But this is not optimism, it is denial of reality. It also reflects mankind's reliance on self rather than God; humanists proudly believe mankind's intelligence and technology has gotten us this far so there are no challenges we can't overcome. The humanist religion has blinded people to the many trends indicating that serious consequences loom ahead. When they do consider the trajectory of a trend, they rationalize it away by thinking we've been in bad fixes before and it worked out just fine in the end. What they are not recognizing is that today's economic, cultural, and political trends are more worldwide than they ever have been before. They certainly don't discern that today's developments are setting the stage for what the Bible says is going to happen. So the world's humanists will be caught by surprise and not ready for the time of God's wrath.

13.26 Anarchy

Let us break Their bonds in pieces and cast away Their cords from us. (Psalm 2:3)

There are more and more instances of "protesters" taking violent action seeking to fundamentally change our society. The media is sympathetic with these efforts and even do what they can to fan the flames of civil disobedience giving voice to the lies of community agitators. At its core, these anarchists who oppose the current order of things are really opposed to God's Law since governments are ultimately proxies of God (Romans 13:1-7). Anarchists who think their protests will result in more freedoms are not rational people. In fact, it will be the other way around. The more violent the anarchist protests become, the more totalitarian the government response will have to be in order to restore order. Since we are headed to totalitarianism during the Tribulation, expect more anarchists organizing riots.

13.27 Inviting God's Judgment

Woe to those who call evil good, and good evil; who put darkness for light, and light for darkness; who put bitter for sweet, and sweet for bitter! (Isaiah 5:20)

Our society turning away from God will bear a bitter fruit. When people reject God's Law, their morality becomes relative to what whoever is in power says it is. Liberal human interpretation of the law changes based on the circumstances and foreshadows what the Antichrist will do per Daniel 7:25. So as we get closer to the Tribulation, we can expect more slandering the good and promoting the evil which only serves to build up God's wrath for the Day of Judgment.

13.28 Drug Use

They did not repent of their murders or their sorceries (Revelation 9:21)
The Greek word translated *"sorceries"* here is pronounced *"pharmakeia"* which refers to drug use. People will be so consumed with taking drugs to medicate reality away during the Tribulation that it gets a mention in the book of Revelation. We can see the stage being set for this today as more people abuse drugs and with increasing efforts to legalize marijuana. Anyone who looks at U.S. incarceration statistics can see that we have lost the so-called war on drugs. The illicit drug business coupled with a culture of corruption has made Mexico a terrible place to live driving millions of refugees into the United States. We can expect drug abuse to get worse as more birth pangs of the Tribulation materialize.

13.29 Drunkenness

We should live soberly, righteously, and godly in the present age, looking for the blessed hope and glorious appearing of our great God and Savior Jesus Christ (Titus 2:12-13)
Another way people seek to escape the reality of this world is over-drinking. Many people would rather go through life impaired than to face the cold harsh truth about this world. Being intoxicated keeps people from living a life that honors God and it means they are not watching for the return of Christ. Those who drink too much will be caught by surprise by the return of the Lord. Unfortunately, as we see more birth pangs of the Tribulation, way too many people will see them as an excuse to get plastered.

13.30 Gambling

Those who want to get rich fall into temptation and a trap and into many foolish and harmful desires that plunge people into ruin and destruction (1 Timothy 6:9, NIV)
It used to be in the United States that if you wanted to gamble, you had to go to either Las Vegas or Atlantic City. But now, virtually every convenience store in the nation offers government sanctioned lottery tickets. Back when the lottery was being debated in Ohio a bumper sticker said, "Lottery: a tax on the mathematically chal-

lenged." It is that and more; making it easy to gamble facilitates people loving money and robs them of what they have earned. Gambling is responsible for breaking up families and is an indicator of the spiritually bankrupt condition of society. More and more people have a debased mind thinking that coming by more money is a matter of "luck" and not the result of working for it.

13.31 Prostitution

Do not prostitute your daughter, to cause her to be a harlot, lest the land fall into harlotry, and the land become full of wickedness (Leviticus 19:29)

Another indicator of a nation's moral condition of is how they regard prostitution. Since the trend is to legitimize vices as we get closer to the return of Christ, we can expect prostitution to become more pervasive and legitimized. The legalization of prostitution has already begun with government looking the other way and not doing much about it; the argument is, "why should the state get involved with what consenting adults do in private?" Eventually the old government argument for allowing vice will be used: "we have to legalize it in order to tax and control it." Legalizing prostitution is a symptom of sexual immorality that will increase as society gets further from God (Romans 1:24, 2 Timothy 3:4).

13.32 Litigation Nation

Wealth gained by dishonesty will be diminished, but he who gathers by labor will increase (Proverbs 13:11)

As we get closer to the lawlessness of the Tribulation we are seeing a proliferation of lawsuits driving up the cost of everything. Most of the growth in lawsuits are frivolous and motivated by greed; people trying to get something out of somebody else. Frivolous lawsuits are nothing but a get-rich-quick scheme. Underlying this trend is a growing moral deficit that comes from society turning away from God.

13.33 Growing Persecution

Jesus said to him, "I am the way, the truth, and the life.
No one comes to the Father except through Me." (John 14:6)

Christians are increasingly being singled out for persecution because of our temerity to claim exclusivity for salvation. The proclamation that a personal relationship with Jesus is the only way to heaven can not be tolerated in this modern age where all opinions must have equal value. Humanists insist on many paths to heaven because that sounds fair and they are all about fairness as they define it. They see the exclusive claims of Christianity as being intolerant which can not be tolerated, circular reasoning notwithstanding. Irrational minds can not see the hypocrisy in that convoluted logic. We can expect to see more Christian persecution birth pangs which reach their peak during the Tribulation, see Matthew 24:9.

13.34 Godless Society Opportunities

They are not of the world, even as I am not of it… As you sent me into the world, I have sent them into the world (John 17:16-18, NIV)

Despite being caught up in the secularization trends, most people instinctively know that society is heading in the wrong direction. As our society gets more and more godless, this actually increases the potential to be a witness for Christ. God called us to be in the world, not of the world. So we should not separate ourselves from the world in Christian enclaves as some suggest because the Lord wants to use us to help more people to come to a saving knowledge of Jesus Christ. The more a Christian is faithful to the Lord, the more they will stand out in our godless culture as something discontented people don't have. Since a godless society foments discontent with the direction of the culture; some people will see where they're headed and will be open to humanism's alternative.

Degenerating Society (2 Timothy 3:1-7)

13.35 Violent

In the last days perilous times will come (2 Timothy 3:1)

The Tribulation will be characterized by wholesale death with half of the planet dying (Revelation 6:8, 9:15). So we should expect to see more violence as the Tribulation draws near. Jesus said that His return would be *"as the days of Noah"* (Matthew 24:37) and we know from Genesis 6:11 that this time was characterized by violence.

13.36 Selfish

For men will be lovers of themselves (2 Timothy 3:2)

People are naturally selfish, but in times past people have been better at masking their selfishness. As we get closer to the Tribulation, we can expect to see more shameless displays of selfishness. What would you expect from people raised to believe they are evolved animals?

13.37 Greedy

Lovers of money (2 Timothy 3:2)

Humanists decry the greed of capitalism arguing that society needs to be more socialist. "Spreading the wealth around" sounds fair but what socialism does is take money from the successful and give it to the lazy. And the administrators of social programs always seem to make out well. So who really are the greedy?

13.38 Prideful

Boasters, proud (2 Timothy 3:2)

Our society is trying to insulate children from failure by not keeping score in sports and passing them on to the next grade no matter what. This has raised up an entire generation of people who have an unrealistically high opinion of themselves. So naturally they act like they are better than everyone else. What they don't realize is that *"pride goes before destruction, and a haughty spirit before a fall"* (Proverbs 16:18). It will not be pretty when this collectively happens in our society as a whole.

13.39 Hateful Toward God

Blasphemers (2 Timothy 3:2)

We have seen the rise of militant atheists who boldly attack Christianity. What better way to lash out at God than to assault His people? It is amazing that people who say they don't believe there is a Creator-God feel so compelled to convince others that their belief is correct. We can expect this spirit of Antichrist to grow as we near the return of Jesus.

13.40 Hateful Toward Parents

Disobedient to parents (2 Timothy 3:2)

A child not respecting their parents by obeying them is commonplace today. Part of this is due to parents adopting a flawed philosophy of permissiveness, but it is also a response to parents not loving their children. Children need structure and discipline; *"He who spares his rod hates his son, but he who loves him disciplines him promptly"* (Proverbs 13:24). It is certainly not politically correct to discipline children today but moving away from biblical principles has consequences within the family and in society as a whole.

13.41 Ungrateful

Unthankful (2 Timothy 3:2)

It seems the more blessings people receive, the less grateful they are to the Giver of blessings (James 1:17). Our culture is moving away from God and has come to believe that the great advances and conveniences we enjoy in modern Western society are due to human achievement. This ungrateful mentality has permeated society fostering an entitlement culture where everyone thinks it is their "right" to more and more benefits. This sinful trend will have consequences.

13.42 Irreverent

Unholy (2 Timothy 3:2)

The humanist worldview has no concept of sin and so society keeps pushing the limits of what used to be considered improper. There used to be swear words that were not used in movies or on television programs but that is no longer the case. The language used is but a symptom of the condition of the culture. Expect our culture to degenerate to even greater depths of vulgarity as we get closer to the Tribulation.

13.43 Hateful

Unloving (2 Timothy 3:3)

We see a lot of hate on display with Islamists trying to eradicate the infidels from wherever they rule. But who does society brand as the haters? It is those who preach the Bible as being literally true. Which is more loving, telling people what they want to hear so they may feel good or telling them the truth so they may make the changes they need to avoid disaster? Those accusing Bible believers of hatred are the true haters and their numbers are growing. Expect hatred of the truth to grow as we get closer to the end of the age.

13.44 Vindictive

Unforgiving (2 Timothy 3:3)

Revenge is growing as a motivation for personal attacks. Humanists have no concept of God making all things right so they feel the need to take justice into their own hands. And man's concept of justice is subject to a flawed perspective when it is not moored to God's Law. A lot of what is called social justice is really just punishing certain groups of people out of some human idea of fairness. Expect more of this as we transition from rule of law to rule of man.

13.45 Politics of Personal Destruction

Slanderers (2 Timothy 3:3)

Leftists can not win intellectually in the marketplace of ideas because their policies do not work and are oppressive rather than empowering. So they always resort to personal destruction as a tactic to distract people from the issues. They will attack their opponent personally to discredit them because they can not win on the validity of their ideological arguments. Expect more personal slander and especially character attacks in politics as the Tribulation nears.

A growing tactic of leftists in the spirit of Antichrist is to accuse people who disagree with them as being old fashioned, unscientific, racist, or haters. This has the impact of shutting down any opposition because people don't want to be accused of these things. Slander puts you on the defensive trying to recover your reputation which only serves to make you look worse. The slanderer rarely gets called on the carpet for their false accusations and it wouldn't matter anyway because the damage has already been done. But justice will be done since God is watching, *"for every idle word men may speak, they will give account of it in the day of judgment"* (Matthew 12:36). Come soon Lord Jesus!

13.46 Undisciplined

Without self-control (2 Timothy 3:3)

The evolutionary worldview says people are just evolved animals. Since animals are not governed by morality, increasingly people likewise are doing whatever they feel like. If there is no ultimate judgment for people, why not do whatever feels good? The problem is that God is just and there will be a reckoning for what people say and do (Matthew 12:36). As people move further from God, they sear their conscience and willfully forget that judgment is coming. So we can expect even more animalistic behavior as the Beast of Revelation draws near.

13.47 Ruthless
Brutal (2 Timothy 3:3)
The evolutionary worldview has survival of the fittest as its engine of change. While the humanist will say we have evolved past the need for survival of the fittest, they still expect it to be a valid path for progress. They'll justify their ruthlessness by saying, "you can't make an omelet without breaking some eggs." When you have no moral mooring, there is no problem with using brutality as a tactic to achieve your goals especially since this is what happens in the survival of the fittest. So expect brutality to increase as mankind turns further from God.

13.48 Evil
Despisers of good (2 Timothy 3:3)
We live in an era when what is good and right is being condemned as being bad and wrong. This is being done to condition people to embrace selfish expression as not being a problem. *"Woe to those who call evil good, and good evil; who put darkness for light, and light for darkness; who put bitter for sweet, and sweet for bitter!"* (Isaiah 5:20). It is the spirit of Antichrist that seeks to change what God has told us is right and wrong (Daniel 7:25). So we can expect to see more people hating what is right and good the closer we get to the rise of the Antichrist.

13.49 Disloyal
Traitors (2 Timothy 3:4)
When people reject the authority of God, they also reject any authority God establishes. Thus people will be disloyal to their employers and governments so that more traitors will emerge. Indeed, this has already become a tool of those with a globalist vision forcing national sovereignty to yield to the new world order. So we can expect more embarrassing national secrets to be exposed publicly. After all, why do we need national secrets if we are to have a global government? Mighty spiritual forces are guiding us ever closer to a worldwide government.

13.50 Arrogant
Headstrong, haughty (2 Timothy 3:4)
At its core, the humanist worldview fosters arrogance. It is the height of arrogance to take credit for what God has done replacing it with

human achievement. This haughty attitude will manifest itself in all manners of human endeavors. It causes formerly democratic governmental leaders to act contrary to public opinion. The pursuit of their ideology takes precedence over what is collectively considered right. As totalitarianism approaches, expect to see political leaders acting more as dictators than governors.

13.51 Hedonists

Lovers of pleasure rather than lovers of God (2 Timothy 3:4)

As more people come to believe that this physical world is all there is, there will be an increasing desire to experience all the pleasures the world offers while there is time. So there will be a growing amount of time and energy going into the pursuit of pleasure. What feels good from a worldly perspective is not necessarily what is good for us particularly when it is taken to excess. God wants us to have pleasure but not without Him. When we recognize that God is the source of our pleasure, we honor Him when we seek it. But the more people pursue pleasure apart from God, the more we kindle His wrath.

13.52 Religious

Having a form of godliness but denying its power (2 Timothy 3:5)

God created us to have a relationship with Him. So when people reject Him, they are compelled to adopt some belief system that takes the place of that relationship. Thus all people have some sort of religion that governs the decisions they make. Humanists reject a personal relationship with God and see themselves as their own authority. They may or may not overtly practice a religion or consider themselves to be spiritual. But they all look to themselves and human institutions as the source of their deliverance rather than Jesus Christ. The further mankind moves away from the power of God, the closer we are to seeing it displayed in God's wrath.

13.53 Exploiters

This sort are those who creep into households and make captives of gullible women loaded down with sins, led away by various lusts (2 Timothy 3:6)

As people move further away from the morality of God, they will seek to achieve their worldly goals any way they can; the end will justify the means. There will be more lying to get ahead and others will be exploited to satisfy worldly pursuits. Indeed people with worldly perspectives are the easiest to exploit and deceivers will use their understanding of common illicit motives to take advantage of them. The more we can train ourselves to have God's eternal perspective, the less susceptible we will be to the growing numbers of exploiters in these end times.

13.54 Egg Heads
Always learning and never able to come to the knowledge of the truth
(2 Timothy 3:7)
Why is it that the most educated among us usually seem to be the furthest from God? Humanists think education can solve all societies' ills without needing a relationship with God, the source of all wisdom. The pursuit of knowledge apart from God will lead a person further from the truth. That is why deception will be so effective in the last days because people will not be spiritually discerning. So expect to see more learned professors pursuing and teaching worthless knowledge *"deceiving and being deceived"* (2 Timothy 3:13).

13.55 Apostasy in the Church
Scoffers will come in the last days, walking according to their own lusts,
and saying, "Where is the promise of His coming?" (2 Peter 3:3-4)
The Church is often a microcosm of society. And this is made worse at the end of this Age as the Church compromises with the world in so many areas. So as your garden variety humanist has no expectation that Jesus Christ will return, neither does your average professing Christian. People don't want the accountability that comes with the imminent return of Christ. They willfully forget that God poured out His wrath on the world once before at the flood and He will do so again before Jesus returns. If it took millions of years from creation to Jesus coming the first time as theistic evolutionists believe, it follows that it will take more millions of years for Him to return. As society continues to degenerate, we should expect to see more of society's problems in the Church. Indeed, this has been prophesied to be the case...

13.56 Doctrines of Demons
Now the Spirit expressly says that in latter times some will depart
from the faith, giving heed to deceiving spirits and doctrines of demons
(1 Timothy 4:1)

As we get closer to the return of Jesus, we can expect a great falling away from faith in Christ among professing Christians. This will be so severe that Jesus posed the question, *"when the Son of Man comes, will He really find faith on the earth?"* (Luke 18:8). During the time leading up to the Lord's return, professing Christians will reject biblical truth and embrace deceptions from fallen angels. Islam, Mormonism, and New Age spirituality are examples of religions proudly proclaiming that they follow the revelation of angels. What they don't realize is that these angels are not speaking for God and are malevolent rather than benevolent.

13.57 Itching Ears

For the time will come when they will not endure sound doctrine,
but according to their own desires, because they have itching ears,
they will heap up for themselves teachers; and they will turn their
ears away from the truth, and be turned aside to fables. (2 Timothy 4:3-4)

Despite living in an age when it is easier to see the fulfillment of Bible prophecy, more professing Christians embrace non-biblical interpretations of Scripture. Most professing Christians today spiritualize Scripture believing it does not necessarily mean what it says. They embrace a spiritual interpretation that they are comfortable with but reject the plain sense reading of the passage. This is particularly the case with Bible prophecy in the embrace of amillennialism; "sure Jesus is returning but not until the end of time which has to be a long, long time away." The idea that time will end is a fable that goes along with other misconceptions of heaven thinking that it is an ethereal spirit world, and this is not something about which us physical beings can get very excited. They also embrace the fable of evolution thinking that God used it as the mechanism of creation. Most Christian seminaries teach these fables cranking out preachers to satisfy their church goers with the feel-good messages they want to hear.

13.58 Laodicean Church

Because you are lukewarm, and neither cold nor hot,
I will vomit you out of My mouth (Revelation 3:16)

It is amazing how the characteristics of the seven churches of Revelation 2:1 – 3:22 parallels church history. Thus the final, Laodicean church characterizes the one on earth at the end of the Age. Indeed, it has gotten harder to find a church that preaches the whole message of the Bible. Most sermons today are the "safe" Christian living messages church goers have come to expect; milk instead of solid food (Hebrews 5:12-14). However, just because most churches during this end of the Age are Laodicean, that does not mean that individual believers have to be lukewarm toward Christ. We can be in the Laodicean Church but not of the Laodicean Church.

13.59 Weak Preaching

They loved the praise of men more than the praise of God (John 12:43)
Preachers in this Laodicean Age seem to avoid the subject of sin; they don't want to offend anyone. Modern preachers have more in common with motivational speakers than they do with pastors of the Church. But the good news of Jesus Christ is offensive to those who have rejected Him (1 Corinthians 1:18). And the message of the cross only makes sense if there are consequences to sin. The problem at the end of the Church Age is not just pastors; it is all believers who will not speak up for Christ to those God brings into their life. The Great Commission is given to all believers, not just pastors.

13.60 Ecumenicalism

All who dwell on the earth will worship him (Revelation 13:8)
During the Tribulation, there will be a global religion with the Antichrist as the collective object of worship. We see birth pangs of this in movements to bring all religions under one umbrella. This has been an objective of the last few Popes and even some prominent evangelical leaders have joined in the effort. Such endeavors are man's attempts to unify the church which only serves to help people be unified under the Antichrist. The Church in this Age is only universal spiritually. But we will be unified physically with the end of the Church Age at the Rapture. Bringing all religions together during the Tribulation is Satan's effort to usurp the worship due God and it will lead many to destruction.

14 POLITICS

Politics is a highly visible derivative of the culture and thus another key indicator of spiritual condition. This chapter makes a case for Christians to be active in politics as good citizens and the most prominent "hot button" politicized issues are discussed from a biblical perspective.

There are a host of issues in the culture that have been politicized to the extent that they merit their own chapter. At their core, all political issues are really spiritual issues. It is hard to debate the merits of one political position versus another without getting into the underlying spiritual perspectives driving a person's opinion. Because strong religions are behind most political viewpoints, some people insist on never even discussing religion or politics in polite company. But it is possible to have a stimulating civil discussion about politics so we should take advantage of our opportunities to do so because such conversations always enable us to plant a seed of spiritual truth that God can use to turn people to Him.

14.1 Political polarization
Since they did not think it worthwhile to retain the knowledge of God,
he gave them over to a depraved mind (Romans 1:28, NIV)
We know that we are close to the return of the Lord because mankind is being given over to a depraved mind of irrationality that makes truth relative to a person's point of view. The vicious partisanship of politics today exhibits this kind of irrational relativity of truth.

And this radical polarization is not just in the United States, it is worldwide as evidenced by the rise of terrorism.

The growth of those with irrational minds is the third stage of God giving mankind over to the consequences of suppressing the truth about Him (Romans 1:18). The first phase where mankind embraced evolution resulted in the break-down of the family and the consequences that came with it (Romans 1:24). The second phase was due to man's growing idolatry and resulted in a plague of homosexuality along with its consequences such as AIDS (Romans 1:26-27).

14.2 Leftists

The heart of the wise inclines to the right, but the heart of the fool to the left.
Even as he walks along the road, the fool lacks sense and shows everyone
how stupid he is. (Ecclesiastes 10:2-3)

Some political views are more aligned with God than others. The Bible makes it clear that a delineation can and should be made between right and wrong. It is interesting that the literal meaning of this passage has relevance for the political situation in our day. Most of the positions held by the politically left are opposed to God: abortion rights, homosexual marriage, militant environmentalism, secularization of society, etc. God does care how we vote.

14.3 Liberal Media

The prince of the power of the air, the spirit who now works
in the sons of disobedience (Ephesians 2:2)

Secular humanism is so pervasive in our society that it has infected most of the media. And most of the news media in the United States no longer serves as an agent restraining evil speaking truth to power. Instead, our reporters and editors appear to be more of a propaganda agency doing all they can to indoctrinate the public in leftist ideology. They do that by outright deception puffing up their leftist politicians while slandering their political opponents. They ignore stories that don't advance their ideology and leave out or change critical details in the stories they can't avoid reporting. They have even manufactured stories to support their leftist narrative because with them, the end justifies the means. It is rare today for news services to verify the facts they report, they just parrot what others have reported previously. The news media in the United States is ready to help the Antichrist deceive the world.

14.4 Voting

Submit yourselves to every ordinance of man for the Lord's sake…
for this is the will of God, that by doing good you may put to silence
the ignorance of foolish men (1 Peter 2:13,15)

Christians are called to be good citizens and one of the responsibilities of a good citizen is to vote. We should vote even when we don't like the choices. There will always be a "lesser evil" to chose and doing our best to slow down the progress of evil in this world honors God. Not voting to *"silence the ignorance of foolish men"* allows them to advance their evil agenda and we all will suffer the resulting consequences. Thus it is better to do what we can by praying and voting even if and especially when we are outnumbered by fools.

14.5 Taking a Stand

Resist the devil and he will flee from you. (James 4:7)

One thing that has caused us to be in the declining condition we are in the U.S. is that God's people have been way too complacent. The devil loves to keep us fat, dumb, and happy not being aware what is happening around us. We'd be better off in this country if God's people were more active in resisting evil as part of our civic responsibilities. Even if we don't like the candidates, we may need to vote against someone rather than for someone. God calls us to take a stand against evil and it honors Him when we obey Him.

14.6 Ungodly Leaders

He removes kings and raises up kings (Daniel 2:21)

God is in control. The government we have has been put in place by God to serve His purposes (Romans 13:1). So when we have an ungodly leader, it is probably a consequence of our ungodly culture; we get the government we deserve. As God raised up Nebuchadnezzar to discipline Judah, He raised up Adolf Hitler to help the world see the need for a Jewish homeland. Ungodly leadership in the U.S. is administering the decline of this country which is necessary to make way for the new global order which the Bible says has to be in place when Jesus returns. All we can do is pray for those in power over us, vote, and speak the truth while we still can; *"I must work the works of*

Him who sent Me while it is day; the night is coming when no one can work" (John 9:4). If our situation helps us and those around us to draw nearer to God, then we know one purpose having ungodly leadership serves.

14.7 Incompetent Leaders

Children are their oppressors, and women rule over them (Isaiah 3:12)
God is in control and He raises up leaders to govern over us to serve His purposes. As God raised up unskilled rulers over Israel as a consequence for the people turning away from Him, we can expect the same thing in our nation. We get the government we deserve. Increasingly today people are not appointed to governmental positions based on their demonstrated character or experience; they are selected for how they look, as a reward for their service, or their loyalty to the boss's ideology. We can expect society to throw out even more of God's values as we get closer to the Tribulation.

14.8 Praying for Leaders

Prayers… for kings and all who are in authority, that we may lead a quiet and peaceable life in all godliness and reverence (1 Timothy 2:1-2)
God raises up the leaders we have for a reason but they are people often under intense pressure and we should pray for them. When our vote doesn't do much more than honor God, praying may be all we can do. A good prayer in situations where we have an ungodly leader doing things that doesn't help us is: *"let his days be few, and let another take his office"* (Psalm 109:8). God is in control and He can raise up a more godly leader.

14.9 Family Values

Be fruitful and multiply (Genesis 1:28)
Leftist ruling elites seek to break down traditional family values because the family is the fundamental building block of a functional society. If society can be sufficiently corrupted, then people will more readily embrace the totalitarian control the ruling elite secretly want to impose on the public.

14.10 Abortion is Murder

For you created my inmost being; you knit me together in my mother's womb. (Psalm 139:13, NIV)

Life begins in the womb at conception. The truth of this is even more obvious with the technology we have today allowing pre-mature babies to survive earlier in their term. Also, 3-D ultrasound imaging makes it clear that pre-born babies have all the physical characteristics of humans very early in their development. Today's technology reveals that it is a baby growing in the mother's womb, not some potentially malignant growth that the term "fetus" conjures up. Babies in the womb have their own distinct DNA even at conception, different from the mother. Abortion is not cutting out an unwanted tumor; it is killing an unborn child. Those who seek to exercise their choice to not take their baby to term really don't care about the impact this has on another human being, their own convenience trumps that.

14.11 Abortion is Avoiding Responsibility

Our fathers sinned and are no more, and we bear their punishment.
(Lamentations 5:7)

Wrong actions always have consequences, even sex outside of marriage. The consequences of sin go beyond the original perpetrator hurting many other people. As we struggle in a fallen world due to our ancestors, our own sin hurts our descendants. There is no "right" to an abortion. Killing an unborn baby to avoid an unwanted child is not taking responsibility. Wrong actions have consequences usually in this world and always in eternity. It is to our credit and God will bless us when we accept responsibility for our own actions.

14.12 God Hates Abortion

The LORD hates… hands that shed innocent blood (Proverbs 6:16-17)

Abortion is taking the life of an innocent baby that is in the world through no fault of its own. God hates this and will visit His wrath on those who engage in it. While God hates the sin of abortion, He still loves the sinner. But that does not mean the sinner is exempt from the consequences of their sin; God is just and there must be a reckoning. But there is hope for all us sinners: *"repent, then, and turn to God, so that your sins may be wiped out, that times of refreshing may come from the Lord"* (Acts 3:19, NIV). Jesus saves those who repent of sin. There is no sin that God can't deliver us from; we simply have to turn to Him for our salvation.

14.13 Evolution Justifies Abortion

For since the creation of the world His invisible attributes are clearly seen, being understood by the things that are made, even His eternal power and Godhead, so that they are without excuse (Romans 1:20)

Devaluing pre-born human life is part of an evolutionary worldview that considers people to be no more than evolved animals. Thus killing some for the convenience of others can be justified since survival of the fittest is the engine that makes evolution work. If life developed by evolution, then survival of the fittest has to be considered a good thing. It is obvious why the theory of evolution was so embraced when Darwin suggested it; thinking of people as just animals can be used to justify all manner of selfish actions.

14.14 Embryonic Stem Cell Research

"Before I formed you in the womb I knew you" (Jeremiah 1:5)

To obtain embryonic stem cells, it is necessary to conceive a baby then abort him or her. This practice devalues human life because it considers newly conceived babies to be expendable. God made clear what He thinks of abortion in Exodus 21:22-25 where He authorized the death penalty for even accidental abortions.

14.15 Abortion Activism

"Vengeance is Mine, I will repay," says the Lord (Romans 12:19)

How should we regard people who try to stop abortion providers by killing them? They are committing as egregious a sin as those who kill babies. God is just and He will see that justice is done. Instead, we should pray for those who facilitate abortions and work to help them to know Jesus as their personal Savior. As good citizens, we should use the legal means at our disposal to end abortions.

It is right to use how a candidate stands on abortion as a "litmus test" as to whether to vote for them or not. Of course this issue must be part of the overall mix of the issues but it is usually the case that people who favor "a woman's right to choose" to murder her unborn baby will also support a myriad of other ungodly policies.

14.16 Population Decline

Children are a heritage from the LORD, the fruit of the womb is a reward (Psalm 127:3)

Once upon a time, having a lot of children was an asset to a family. That is no longer the case in modern Western Civilization; having children is now considered a liability. Having more than one child was even outlawed in China. Such a mentality is a product of the humanism that permeates this age. Thinking only of the limited resources to support more children, modern humanists don't bother to consider that a larger population can produce more resources. People turning to their own uninspired solutions rather than to the Provider will kindle God's wrath and thus is a sign of the times.

14.17 Abortion is a Sign of the Times

The earth also was corrupt before God, and the earth was filled with violence (Genesis 6:11)

Jesus said one of the signs of the time leading up to His return would be, *"as the days of Noah were"* (Matthew 24:37). Those days where characterized by violence. It is hard to imagine that there could have been more murders in the day of Noah than the innocent lives that have been taken in the United States since Roe versus Wade. There will be consequences to our violent ways.

14.18 Gay Marriage

A man will leave his father and mother and be united to his wife,
and they will become one flesh. (Genesis 2:24, NIV)

The problem with homosexual marriage is that it attempts to bring an aura of acceptability to a practice condemned in Scripture. At the same time it attacks the natural order diluting the value of an institution established by God. If any two people or group of people can enter into a covenant called marriage, why even bother to marry? Breaking down institutions established by God is in the spirit of Antichrist.

14.19 Gay Gene

Let no one say when he is tempted, "I am tempted by God"; for God cannot
be tempted by evil, nor does He Himself tempt anyone. (James 1:13)

While there is no scientific proof of a gay gene, people persist in believing that gay people are born that way. That is why the gay lobby insists on their issues being treated like civil rights. It is as if being gay is a physical characteristic they can do nothing about. Being gay is a behavior, and behaviors can be changed. People are not born with a propensity to be gay. Environmental factors no-doubt contribute to a desire to be gay but it is still a choice. An evolutionary worldview helps justify homosexuality; if we are just evolved animals, why not just give into our animalistic urges?

14.20 Gay Sign of the Times

God gave them over to shameful lusts. (Romans 1:26, NIV)
In Romans 1:18-32 we see three phases of God giving mankind over to the consequences of his sin. Mainstreaming homosexuality in the culture is the second phase. While we are now well into the third phase of irrationality; the second phase has completely metastasized. People now fear offending gay people and it is increasingly demanded that all people embrace the gay lifestyle. If you don't join in proclaiming that being gay is normal and natural, you are accused of committing a hate crime. Christians are targeted in particular trying to get them to deny what the Bible says about sodomy. How a person stands on gay issues is now a litmus test on whether you are sufficiently progressive in your ideology or are among the Luddites holding society back.

14.21 Gay Plague

Men committed indecent acts with other men, and received in themselves
the due penalty for their perversion. (Romans 1:27, NIV)
It is not politically correct to acknowledge that AIDS is primarily spread by men in the gay lifestyle. But this is hard to deny if you look at honest statistics. The gay lobby tries to position their lifestyle as just an alternative to the monogamous man-woman relationship that is marriage but in actuality homosexuality is usually also characterized by promiscuity. AIDS could be quickly wiped out if society got serious about biblical morality. AIDS should shake us up about immoral lifestyles and the fact that we can not eradicate it reveals society's stage of decay.

14.22 Days of Lot

Likewise as it was also in the days of Lot: They ate, they drank, they bought,
they sold, they planted, they built; but on the day that Lot went out of Sodom
it rained fire and brimstone from heaven and destroyed them all.
(Luke 17:28-29)

Jesus makes reference to *"the days of Lot"* as a statement on the condition of society in the time-frame of His return. Genesis 19 tells the story of Sodom where homosexuality was rampant in their culture. Thus we can expect gay issues to be a greater part of our culture as we get closer to the Tribulation. The pervasiveness of the gay culture worldwide is a significant sign of the times.

14.23 Hope for Gays

Do not be deceived. Neither fornicators, nor idolaters, nor adulterers, nor homosexuals, nor sodomites… will inherit the kingdom of God. And such were some of you. But you were washed, but you were sanctified, but you were justified in the name of the Lord Jesus and by the Spirit of our God.
(1 Corinthians 6:9-11)

We are all sinners and homosexual behavior is no worse sin than any other immoral behavior. Jesus died to make it possible for all our sins to be forgiven. The only unforgivable sin is unbelief (Matthew 12:31-32). We all have our own compulsions that we struggle with in our mortal lives but God gives us strength to resist our temptations (1 Corinthians 10:13). Jesus delivers those who repent by acknowledging their sin and commit themselves to turning away from it with God's help.

14.24 Gay Hate

Love your enemies, bless those who curse you, do good to those who hate you, and pray for those who spitefully use you and persecute you (Matthew 5:44)

Gay activists hate Christians because the Bible condemns the behavior that defines them. They think Christians must hate them as well but don't understand that God enables us to hate the sin while loving the sinner. Indeed as humanists, gay people don't even recognize their behavior as sin. The hatred gay activists have for Bible believers will be one of the engines for persecution of Christians as we get closer to the return of Christ. Ultimately this hatred is directed against God. Gay activists can't hurt God so they seek to hurt His people. While it is human nature to return hatred for hatred, this is something Christians know to leave to God; *"'Vengeance is Mine, I will repay,' says the Lord."* (Romans 12:19).

14.25 Hate Crime Law

You shall know the truth, and the truth shall make you free (John 8:32)

Humanists are trying to make it a crime to speak about certain things such as what the Bible says about homosexuality. Eventually they will outlaw the Bible which has been attempted in many places before. This stifling of free speech is unconstitutional in the United States but the day will come when the ruling elites are successful in suspending our constitutional rights. We know that will be the case during the Tribulation when there is a totalitarian world government under the Antichrist. The purpose of hate crime laws is to cause Christians to stop speaking the truth of the Scriptures. Their efforts to shut us up should give us an urgency to, *"work the works of Him who sent Me while it is day; the night is coming when no one can work"* (John 9:4)

14.26 Feminism

Your desire will be for your husband, and he will rule over you (Genesis 3:16)

God made men and women differently and gave them different roles in the family and, by extension, society. As was foretold about Eve, women will naturally covet the role God has given men and this will cause tension between men and women. At this advanced stage of history, men have yielded more of their traditional roles to women and society is now seeing the consequences of this. Career women are depriving children of their mothers and men of their wives. Men have gotten lazy and shirked their responsibilities. There are more broken families and children growing up not knowing how they should conduct themselves before God. Feminism is just one more thing in this world that shows us we need the Messiah to return.

14.27 Victimhood; Avoiding Responsibility

Each one shall bear his own load (Galatians 6:5)

The root cause of societies' ills is not taking responsibility for our own bad choices. This makes everyone a victim of something beyond their control; racism, poverty, bad education, or even poor toilet training. The real problem in our society is a spiritual one where people deny God's authority in their lives. Not taking responsibility goes all the way back to Adam and Eve when they disobeyed God then both blamed someone else. Adam blamed *"the woman You gave to be with me"* and Eve blamed it on Satan (Genesis 3:12-13).

The world system Satan established is one where there is no concept of sin. Thus society falsely believes that human nature is basically good. What then is a person to do if they don't know that their sin is the cause for their bad choices? They think it can't be their fault, so they convince themselves their problems must be due to someone or something else. However, God's Word says it is really our nature to be bad, *"all have sinned and fall short of the glory of God"* (Romans 3:23). Only trusting in Jesus Christ can keep us from the ultimate consequences of our sin nature (Romans 6:23).

14.28 Political Correctness

The stone which the builders rejected has become the chief cornerstone,
and a stone of stumbling and a rock of offense (1 Peter 2:7-8)

Political correctness ostensibly tries to avoid offending some group of people. Among the most egregious applications of political correctness in our day is not acknowledging the source of Islamic terrorism. In an effort to avoid offending any Muslims, our society can not bring itself to admit that the problem is the Islamic religion. So consequently, no one has a clue about how to deal with the growing terrorism problem. If the media would only ostracize Islam as an evil culture half as much as they do Christianity, we'd find there are fewer people jumping on the jihad bandwagon. But they can not bring themselves to do this so Islamic terrorism will continue to get worse. You can't fight something if you can't even name the enemy in order to attack the root of the problem.

The only belief system political correctness doesn't seek to avoid offending is Christianity. That is because people who don't want to be accountable to the Creator-God find the good news of Jesus Christ to be offensive. The exclusive nature of being a child of God is certainly offensive to those who reject Him. Such being offended by the Truth will be one of the engines of Christian persecution during the Tribulation. As Jesus said, *"if they persecuted Me, they will also persecute you"* (John 15:20).

14.29 Racism

There is no partiality with God (Romans 2:11)

The apostles had to deal with racial conflict between the Jews and Gentiles in the early church. However, God, *"made no distinction between us and them, purifying their hearts by faith"* (Acts 15:9). God revealed this to the church through Peter who said, *"in truth I perceive that God shows no partiality."* (Acts 10:34 and 1 Peter 1:17) Paul taught the gospel to both Jews and Gentiles, *"for it is the power of God to salvation for everyone who believes"* (Romans 1:16).

Paul also taught that since God didn't make distinctions between the races, then neither should we (Romans 2:11, Ephesians 6:9, and Colossians 3:25). James said that having prejudices about people different from us was sin (James 2:1-9). The agape love of Christ in us should help us avoid the *"evil thoughts"* that come with prejudices and become the rationalizations for racism (James 2:4). When we have prejudices, we judge the motivation of others which is sin, *"for in whatever you judge another you condemn yourself; for you who judge practice the same things."* (Romans 2:1; see also James 4:11-12)

If we are true followers of Christ, we will obey his command to, *"make disciples of all the nations"* regardless of race (Matthew 28:19). All races will be represented in heaven, *"out of every tribe and tongue and people and nation"* (Revelation 5:9). Genesis 1:26 tells us that all people were created in the image of God. *"Have we not all one Father? Has not one God created us? Why do we deal treacherously with one another by profaning the covenant of the fathers?"* (Malachi 2:10).

Despite the Bible's admonitions to not have prejudices about different races, racism rages on in the world. Indeed as we see more racism being stirred up, this is a sign we are getting close to the Tribulation. Jesus Christ cited racial strife as one of the signs of His soon return in Matthew 24:7, *"For nation will rise against nation, and kingdom against kingdom."* The Greek word from the original text translated *"nation"* is *"ethnos"* which means a people or race.

14.30 Death Penalty

Whoever sheds the blood of man, by man shall his blood be shed;
for in the image of God has God made man. (Genesis 9:6, NIV)

It is too bad that we have to have a death penalty. But as long as there are murderers on the earth, there needs to be consequences for their evil actions. Governments have been ordained to act for God in maintaining order and that includes making sure there are consequences for murder. Humanists seek to end the death penalty because they really want to see an end of God's Law. They are actually seeking lawlessness and this reveals their spirit of Antichrist.

Sure governments sometimes make mistakes and execute the wrong person. But in general, our due process has sufficient checks and balances to make this very rare. It is no reason to throw the baby out with the bath water. Excusing murderers as being victims contributes to the degeneration of society to cause even more murders. Eventually, when society gets corrupt enough, a totalitarian government will be required to restore order. This is the ultimate goal of the anti-death penalty crowd whether they acknowledge it or not.

14.31 Gun Control

If anyone does not provide for his own, and especially for those of his household, he has denied the faith and is worse than an unbeliever (1 Timothy 5:8)

It is true that, "if guns are outlawed, only outlaws will have guns." In the irrational liberal mind, having guns around is the problem that has to be solved in order to reduce gun violence. But these liberals are just the "useful idiots" of the ruling elite who seek to enhance their power by imposing more control over the public. The reason we have a Second Amendment in the U.S. is so that people are not totally dependant on the government for their personal self-defense. The police can't be everywhere all the time. But the ruling class who desires totalitarian control can not allow us to defend ourselves taking every opportunity to whittle away at our freedoms to make people more dependant on the centralized control authority.

14.32 Separation of Church and State

He will speak against the Most High and oppress His saints and try to change the set times and the laws (Daniel 7:25, NIV)

It is no longer politically correct to display a memorial of the Ten Commandments at government buildings. The spirit of Antichrist is behind removing public prayer from schools, displays of the Ten Commandments from courtrooms, calling Christmas a generic winter celebration, and other trends secularizing society. Historical revisionism about the Christian origins of the U.S. is taking place to indoctrinate children into the ways of a utopian godless society. Since the spirit of Antichrist is driving this historical revisionism, we can expect more of it. What Antichrist devotees don't realize is the more they try to suppress God's Word, the more people will turn to Him because truth resonates louder during times of persecution. Make no mistake, trying to "protect the public" from exposure to all Christian expression is a forerunner of persecution.

15 THE FULLNESS OF TIME

The fullness of time has enabled us to better understand that we are now in the season of Christ's return. The concept of 1,000 years being as a day to God helps us to see that we are in the time-frame for the return of Jesus. The Parable of the Fig Tree, the command to restore Jerusalem, and the biblical concept of Jubilee all reinforce that the return of Christ has to be near.

While we can not know the day or hour that Jesus will return (Matthew 25:13), we can know the season because Jesus gave us signs for which to watch. Some day soon the time will be right for His return the same as it was for His first coming; *"when the fullness of the time had come, God sent forth His Son"* (Galatians 4:4). The first time Jesus came, God prepared the way for the gospel to be disseminated using Greek as a common language of commerce and facilitating travel with Roman roads. Likewise today, God is setting the stage with Israel being back in the land, preparing people to embrace a global government, and technology that will fulfill prophecy.

Besides the signs Jesus gave us to watch for, there are some other indications in Scripture that we are in the season of His return...

15.1 Two Days
Come, and let us return to the LORD; for He has torn, but He will heal us;
he has stricken, but He will bind us up. After two days He will revive us;
on the third day He will raise us up, that we may live in His sight
(Hosea 6:1-2)

The context of Hosea 6:1-2 is the Lord delivering Israel. The reference to the days here best makes sense in light of 2 Peter 3:8 which is relevant because it too is speaking of the time of the Lord's return: *"with the Lord one day is as a thousand years, and a thousand years as one day."* This concept was also understood in Old Testament times: *"For a thousand years in Your sight are like yesterday when it is past, and like a watch in the night"* (Psalm 90:4). Thus the *"two days"* Israel has to wait for deliverance is really 2,000 years. Scholars say Hosea wrote this in about 725 BC. So then, adding 2,000 years to 725 BC is 1276 AD. Thus the *"third day"* is ~1277 to ~2277 AD. According to the Prophet Hosea, we are well into the era of the Lord's return!

15.2 6,000 Years

For in six days the LORD made the heavens and the earth, the sea, and all that is in them, and rested the seventh day. (Exodus 20:11)

This passage can not be properly understood apart from taking a literal, biblical "young earth" view of Scripture. Proponents of theistic evolution would have us believe it was millions of years from creation until the first advent of Christ. Thus there is no reason to expect Him to return any time soon. A literal reading of Scripture and evidence from creation science tells us the earth is much younger.

The genealogy of Jesus Christ all the way back to Adam is given in Luke 3:23-38. We know how many years there were between the generations of the long-living ancestors before the flood because this was given in Genesis 5. Applying a 35 to 40 year gap between the other generations gives us about 2,000 years from Adam to Abraham, and another 2,000 years from Abraham to Jesus. Since we know that it has been about 2,000 years since Jesus, we are at about 6,000 years of human history (give or take a life-span).

Multiple Hebrew sages have commented that they expect there to be 7,000 years of mortal human history that parallel the seven days of creation. As God worked six days and rested on the seventh, mankind will travail for 6,000 years and rest during the last millennium. Certainly Scripture tells us of the 1,000-year Millennial Kingdom in which Jesus, the Prince of Peace, will personally rule on earth thus providing rest from strife between the nations. The 7,000 years of history concept is further reinforced in the fact that the number seven and its multiples have significance in Scripture representing "completion."

Consistent with the Hebrew sages' expectation for human history is the Hebrew "Lunisolar" calendar which is supposed to reflect the number of years it has been since creation. The year 2015 in our Gregorian calendar is roughly equivalent to the year 5775 in the Hebrew calendar. The Lord did not give us enough information to calculate exactly when the creation week happened so there could easily be 250 years of error in what the Hebrew scholars came up with in the First Century. However, the Hebrew Calendar is just one more indication that we are close to 6,000 years of history.

15.3 Parable of the Fig Tree
Now learn this parable from the fig tree: When its branch has already become tender and puts forth leaves, you know that summer is near. So you also, when you see all these things, know that it is near-- at the doors! Assuredly, I say to you, this generation will by no means pass away till all these things take place (Matthew 24:32-34)
We know that the fig tree is a symbol of Israel per Hosea 9:10 and Joel 2:21-25. Jesus told us that there will be people who see Him return who were alive when Israel was re-established (May 14, 1948). And the Bible also tells us how long a generation is: *"the days of our lives are seventy years; and if by reason of strength they are eighty years"* (Psalm 90:10). If 80 years sets the bounds for a generation, then this means that Jesus has to return by 2028 (1948 plus 80 years). But since 70 years also defines a generation, this means that Jesus could return by 2018. And knowing that the Rapture occurs at least seven years prior to the Second Coming of Jesus, we have been in the season of His return since 2011.

15.4 Restoring Jerusalem
From the going forth of the command to restore and build Jerusalem until Messiah the Prince, there shall be seven weeks and sixty-two weeks (Daniel 9:25)
The 69 weeks of years in Daniel or 483 years was fulfilled between Persian King Artaxerxes commanding Jerusalem to be restored until Messiah Jesus was *"cut off"* by dying on the cross (Daniel 9:26). It is biblical that history does repeat itself; *"That which has been is what will be, that which is done is what will be done, and there is nothing new under the sun"* (Ecclesiastes 1:9). So while the 483 years of Daniel applied to the first coming of Jesus, could it also apply to the return of Jesus as a

prophetic type? There was another command to restore Jerusalem by another Gentile king in history. As Artaxerxes of Persia is to the first coming of Christ, Suleiman of the Ottoman Empire is to His second coming. Suleiman the Magnificent ordered the Jerusalem wall to be rebuilt in 1535. Adding 483 years to 1535 gives us 2018. So something pretty significant related to the Second Coming of Christ will likely happen in the time-frame of 2018.

15.5 120th Jubilee

*You shall consecrate the fiftieth year, and proclaim liberty throughout
all the land... It shall be a Jubilee for you* (Leviticus 25:10)

God told us that we should expect to find clues about the end of the age in Genesis; *"Remember the former things of old, for I am God... declaring the end from the beginning"* (Isaiah 46:9-10). Indeed, the Bible has been described as being like a hologram in that the gospel may be seen in any piece of it. Jesus also told us that we should look at the first time God poured out His wrath on earth for clues about His return: *"as the days of Noah were, so also will the coming of the Son of Man be"* (Matthew 24:37).

When God revealed the coming flood to Noah, he was told how long he would have to build the ark: *"My Spirit shall not strive with man forever... his days shall be one hundred and twenty years"* (Genesis 6:3). The 120 years of Genesis may establish for us a pattern to be applied to Israel's ultimate deliverance in the 50-year Jubilee cycle. The Jubilee year occurred every seventh shemitah (sabbatical year) where land and property was returned to the original families that owned it. If we are close to 6,000 years of history, the 120th Jubilee approaches; 120 times 50 equals 6,000 years.

If we are coming up on the 120th Jubilee, we should expect to see some critical developments 50-years apart in Israel's history representing the 119th and 118th Jubilees. Two events stand out that fit this: (1) The Balfour Declaration of 1917 ended the centuries-long rule of the Ottoman Empire over the land of Israel and laid the foundation for establishing "a national home for the Jewish people." (2) Israel took over control of Jerusalem in 1967 as a result of the Six-Day War. That this war was concluded in six days attests to God's work since it is tied to God's work of creation.

If 1917 and 1967 were the 118th and 119th Jubilees, then the 120th Jubilee would be in 1967 plus 50 equals 2017. Since the Hebrew calendar does not line up exactly with our Gregorian calendar, this could easily be 2018, the same year the Parable of the Fig Tree and the 483 years of Daniel both also point to; coincidence? Those who know our Almighty God don't believe in coincidences.

15.6 Our Response

Do business till I come (Luke 19:13)

Since we are clearly in the season of the Rapture, should we quit our jobs and gather on a mountain to wait for Jesus? God places us where we are for a reason, we certainly can keep watch for Jesus to return from anywhere. Recognizing the season we are in we just need to be ready; and do what we can to help others to know the Lord so that they may join us in the Rapture. It certainly doesn't look like we have long to persevere in this world.

15.7 Time is Short

Now it is high time to awake out of sleep; for now our salvation is nearer than when we first believed. (Romans 13:11)

The message for believers is to get on with what God has called us to do. We should take full advantage of the times to help others see what the Bible says is really happening. Unbelievers need to see this as a wake-up call and respond to that seed of faith God has given them, repent of their sin, and start trusting in Jesus as their Savior and Lord for everything before it is too late.

15.8 Believe

God so loved the world that He gave His only begotten Son, that whoever believes in Him should not perish but have everlasting life. (John 3:16)

Jesus came into our world to reveal the love of God to us by paying the penalty for our sins. He has done everything necessary for our salvation. All we do to appropriate His provision for us is respond to Him by believing. To believe is to recognize that Jesus Christ is the Almighty Creator God, to trust in His shed blood on the cross as full payment for our sins, and acknowledge that He rose from the dead. Our response to Him in believing is the initial step of faith associated with the miraculous transformation of our human spirits so that we may begin to understand spiritual matters. This initiates the eternal relationship with our Creator that He intends for us and we may grow in that relationship as we pursue fellowship with Him. It is the beginning of an amazing journey.

SCRIPTURE INDEX

TOPIC INDEX

Topic Index

Topic Index

rewards 2.11, 3.9, 3.15, 12.0, 12.1, 14.16

rewards for watching 2.8

rewards, loss of 2.5, 6.3

robotics 12.44

rock dating 11.3

Roman Empire 8.1, 9.16-9.18, 15.0

rule of law 6.3, 6.7-6.9, 13.44

rule of man 6.3, 6.7, 6.9, 6.13, 6.18, 13.44

ruling class 6.23, 7.8, 10.6, 10.12. 10.14, 10.17, 14.31

ruling elites 6.7, 7.8, 10.1, 10.10, 10.16, 14.9, 14.25, 14.31

Russia 3.11, 5.9, 8.4

Sagan, Carl 13.7

salt and light 6.3

salvation 2.2, 2.3, 2.6-2.9, 3.8, 6.3, 13.2, 13.6, 13.33, 14.12, 14.29, 15.7

Satan 2.5, 2.9, 3.6, 3.9, 3.15, 3.17, 4.1, 4.17, 6.1, 6.6, 6.15, 6.20, 7.0, 7.6, 7.7, 8.2, 9.3, 9.4, 9.9, 9.28, 10.9, 10.13, 10.14, 13.3, 13.60, 14.27

Satan, ruler of world 7.6

satellites 11.3, 12.5, 12.40-12.42

Saudi Arabia 5.14, 8.4, 8.16, 9.15

science fiction 2.11, 3.16

science, creation 12.28, 15.2

science, origin of 12.1

scoffers 2.9, 3.0, 13.55

sea, oceans 12.17, 12.18

secularization 7.10, 13.34, 14.2, 14.32

security 5.18, 7.11, 7.13, 8.4, 12.31, 12.32

selfishness 2.10, 4.12, 6.2, 6.10, 13.9, 13.11, 13.20, 13.22, 13.36, 13.48, 14.13

Sharia Law 9.1, 9.24

Sharon, Ariel 8.17

signs 2.8, 3.9, 4.0, 4.14, 12.34, 4.22, 14.17, 14.29, 15.0

signs and wonders 3.16, 4.17, 6.1

signs, astronomical 4.18, 11.4

signs, Israel 5.0

signs, technological 12.34, 12.35

sin 2.4, 2.9, 2.10, 3.4, 3.6, 3.17, 6.1, 6.13, 7.7, 8.2, 10.3, 10.15, 12.14, 13.9, 13.42, 14.11, 14.12, 14.15, 14.23, 14.24, 14.27, 14.29

Six-Day War 5.11, 15.5

skeptics 2.0, 2.1, 3.19, 5.10, 8.1, 11.4, 13.16

slander 6.15, 13.27, 13.45, 14.3

social justice 6.3, 6.13, 13.44

socialism, biblical 10.2

socialism, destruction 6.23, 10.9, 10.11

socialism, failure of 10.3, 10.7, 10.10, 13.37

socialism, growing 4.1, 6.22, 6.23, 10.0, 10.1, 10.6, 10.16, 13.14

sovereignty, yield of 3.12, 6.3, 7.0, 7.3, 7.8, 11.7, 13.49

Soviet Union 6.3, 7.0

space 3.6, 12.4, 12.6, 12.9, 12.11, 12.12, 12.40

Spain 8.1, 8.4, 10.12

Sudan 8.4

Suleiman 15.4

supernatural 1.0, 3.2, 3.6, 3.14, 4.13, 4.17, 5.7, 8.4, 8.21, 12.1, 12.34, 12.36, 12.41, 12.42

survival of the fittest 2.4, 13.13, 13.47, 14.13

survival of the species 13.14

survivalist 2.9, 3.7

Syria 5.9, 5.14, 8.4-8.6, 9.2, 9.16, 9.17, 9.23

taqiyya 9.5

ABOUT THE AUTHOR

Scott Huckaby became a Christian upon discovering that Bible prophecy made sense of the perplexing end of the Cold War in 1991. He has been an adult Bible study teacher at Southern Baptist and nondenominational churches since 1994 and a supply preacher in the San Felipe and Big Bend Baptist Associations. He holds a Bachelor of Science degree in electrical engineering from the University of Cincinnati, was a U.S. Army officer and worked 27 years as a Product Marketing Engineer at Texas Instruments. Readers can connect with Scott Huckaby through his blog: newswisdom.blogspot.com.

Made in the USA
San Bernardino, CA
08 December 2017